Mine to Do

Responding to Race-Based Hatred and Violence

Tracy Brown

www.WhatIsMineToDo.com

Mine to Do: Responding to Race-Based Hatred and Violence

ISBN13:   978-1-889819-44-0
ISBN10:   1-889819-44-1

brown bridges press
PO Box 12866, Dallas Texas 75225

Dedication

This book is dedicated to my friend and colleague, Patti Digh. She asked herself the question "What is mine to do?" then answered it in an amazing and life-changing way.

A Personal Message from Tracy Brown

This collection is simply the sharing of thoughts and emotions related to the topic of race-based hatred and violence.

It is not designed to convince you that race-based hatred and violence is wrong. But if you are already committed to creating a society, workplace or spiritual community where respect and fairness are the norm, you will find information and inspiration to encourage and empower you.

You may already be aware of the Facebook Group: What Is Mine to Do. If not, join us there and share your tips and ideas with others on the journey.

Visit WhatIsMineToDo.com for inspirational quotations and other posts that will help you identify actions you might take to replace race-based hatred and violence with respect and fairness. There is a link to the "What Is Mine to Do" TEDxSMU talk there as well.

Tracy Brown
www.WhatIsMineToDo.com

Other Books by Tracy Brown

What Is Mine to Do Journal

Make Your Cross-Cultural Conversations Productive: 10 Guidelines

71 Ways to Inspire Commitment to Diversity and Inclusion

71 Ways to Demonstrate Commitment to Diversity and Inclusion

You Are Young, Gifted and Black: Wisdom from Your Ancestors

Breaking the Barrier of Bias: The Subtle Influence of Bias and What to Do About It

Leaderthink: Inspiring Reminders to Think – and Act – Like a Leader, Volume 1

Leaderthink: Inspiring Reminders to Think – and Act – Like a Leader, Volume 2

Table of Contents

In response to race-based hatred and violence ...

WhatIsMineToDo.com

Join the Facebook Group: What Is Mine To Do

Mine to Do

Responding to Race-Based Hatred and Violence

Tracy Brown

WhatIsMineToDo.com

Foreword

Race-based hatred. Race-based violence.

So many people I talked to were desperate for conditions to change. But they were equally frustrated that the institutions and organizations they were a part of didn't seem to have a sense of urgency.

So I started making a simple request:

> "Complete this sentence: In response to race-based hatred and violence I will: _____."

At first there were hesitant responses. Often people responded with, "What do you mean what will I do? It's the police that need to change." or "Me ... I'm just one person; I can't change anything."

I persisted. I reminded people that each one of us comes into contact with dozens, if not hundreds of people in our daily lives. I asked, "What if each one of us simple set a good example of no longer accepting race-based hatred or violence to go unchallenged in our own lives?"

Of course, there also were people who were *excited* about holding themselves accountable for doing something right in their own life. It felt energizing, necessary, exciting or important to take matters into their own hands.

So, "What is Mine to Do" is all about individuals from all identity groups doing what they can with the people they meet in the places they go.

Let's shift the paradigm. Let's make it clear that race-based hatred and violence is not okay. Let's demonstrate that race-based hatred and violence can be stopped: one person, one family, one neighborhood, one workspace, one restaurant, one conversation at a time.

First Person Plural

Have you heard (or said) statements like these?

> *"I just found my soul mate ... we finish each other's sentences."*

> *"My best friend and I like the same things, have the same sense of humor and are just so much alike!"*

> *I love working with John; we agree on just about everything."*

I'm sure you get the point. We often prefer being around people who we perceive to be just like us ... or at least so much like us that we don't really have to extend any effort to understand them (or to be understood).

Unfortunately, that's not how it is at work and in many other settings we find ourselves in on a regular basis.

Defining "We"

In the Merriam-Webster dictionary, the word "we" is defined as:

> *"I and the rest of a group that includes me: you and I: you and I and another or others: I and another or others not including you —used as pronoun of the first person plural"*

We is a pronoun that is "first person plural." It's not "one person plural" (which would be multi-personality disorder). It's not "same person plural" (which would be cloning).

First person plural means there are a group of people who are engaged together in some task or activity. First person plural means there is a group of people who act as one or who choose to share an identity. But it doesn't mean they are all the same.

Unity Not Uniformity

We is a word that indicates there is a common thread that connects people who are each unique but, for some reason, have joined together to share an experience.

Need I use a most obvious example?

> *"We the People of the United States, in Order to form a more perfect Union, establish Justice, insure domestic Tranquility, provide for the common defence, promote the general Welfare, and secure the Blessings of Liberty to ourselves and our Posterity, do ordain and establish this Constitution for the United States of America."*

This Preamble to the Constitution of the United States provides a great reminder that differences exist AND we can choose to join together with those who are different from us in many ways but have a shared role, goal or watering hole.

Look in the Mirror

So this week at work, or in your community, take a look around. Are you surrounded by near-duplicate versions of yourself? Or do you surround yourself with people who are different in many ways?

Do you tend to identify with "we" as being engaged with many versions of yourself? Or do you experience "we" as a kaleidoscope of differences coming together for a common good?

You and I are different. And unique. And valuable.

Let's combine our talents, our gifts, our perceptions and our experiences in order to demonstrate the powerful transformational journey from "me and you" to "we."

"We've got to learn somehow to respect ourselves without having to put someone else down."

Bill Hohri

Join the Facebook Group: What Is Mine To Do

What is Mine to Do?

So this morning I reported for jury duty. Sitting in the courtroom, waiting to be called, I had plenty of time to consider this question:

---

*What if I were selected to serve on the jury
of the young white man who shot and killed
black people in a prayer meeting just
because of the color of their skin?*

There was an empty chair between me and the middle aged white man to my left so I was slightly surprised when I felt his hand touch my arm as he whispered,

"Are you okay? Is there anything I can do?"

I hadn't realized I was crying until that moment. I wiped my face, took a breath, then turned to him and said,

*"Thanks for asking. And yes. What you can
do is tell everyone you know that you, as a
white man, think it's time for white people
to stop killing black people just because of
the color of their skin."*

Luckily, he didn't run screaming from the room. And he didn't think I was completely crazy. We had a thoughtful conversation about the difference between feeling bad about what has happened to strangers and speaking up about what is unacceptable for anyone and everyone. We talked about the distinction between taking action and being an activist.

We agreed that we all need to ask the question,

"What is mine to do?"

And then take some positive action. Every one of us can take a positive action with the people we come in contact with. We all touch dozens (if not hundreds or thousands) of lives every week. We all have our own individual sphere of influence.

It is no surprise that black people speak up and speak out when hatred, racism and violence result in death of innocent African Americans. But when black people speak out it is often characterized as whining, self-serving or complaining. It is still ridiculously rare for white people in America to take a personal stand on these issues beyond an expression of sorrow or pity for the families of those people far away in that other community where something unfortunate happened.

But the reality is this. White people are the ones who have to say to other white people that the hatred, violence and killing must stop.

- White police officers have to say to other white officers that it is not okay to hide behind the excuse that they feared for their lives when they are the ones who are armed and trained to handle any conflict that arises.

- White executives must be the ones to say to white managers that it is no longer acceptable to claim a white candidate is a better "fit" for the job simply

10

because they have more in common with the white candidate or are less comfortable with the equally or better qualified African American candidate.

- White coworkers must be the ones to say to their white colleagues that the racially based joke wasn't funny or that reference to the noose was offensive.

- White journalists have to be the ones to put a stop to their colleagues labeling similar behavior and circumstances differently depending on the race of the people being described.

Speaking up and taking a stand does not require you to go to a protest rally or get on national TV or quit your job and become a full-time advocate for peace and justice. Speaking up and taking a stand simply requires you to choose fairness and equity in every way possible in your own sphere of influence.

If we don't stop this now, what kind of world and workplace will we leave for the generations coming behind us? Hatred is carefully taught and cowardly tolerated. Our future is hopeless if we fail to do what is ours to do now to end this pattern.

As a black woman I will keep speaking up when I see us failing to live up to the values and principles described in our nation's founding documents. As an expert on diversity and inclusion in the workplace it is my responsibility to continue educating and encouraging equity, respect and curiosity. As a baby boomer, it is important for me to take action now to help the world evolve into a place that is safe for my 20-year old God-daughter, her friends and the generations coming behind her.

As far as the stranger I met this morning, I hope, when he returns to his workplace, his family, his church and his neighborhood, that he will let it be known he is no longer willing to be silent about dangerous and disrespectful treatment of people of color.

What about you? What is yours to do to help shift us away from tolerating the effects of racism that lead to violence, death or inequity? Post what you are willing to do anywhere on social media, and use the hashtag #minetodo. Let's create some momentum for meaningful change.

Remember the world changes one person, one conversation and one relationship at a time.

Tracy Brown

Join the Facebook Group: What Is Mine To Do

"Thoughts are like arrows: once released, they strike their mark. Guard them well or one day you may be your own victim."

Navajo Proverb

Join the Facebook Group: What Is Mine To Do

One Week Later ... Now What?

- Nine people killed for no reason other than their race.
- Nine people murdered in a church, a place that most consider both the safest and most sacred refuge from the stress and confusion of our world.
- Nine people giving us the gift of shocking millions out of complacency and comfort.
- Millions of people are asking "What is Mine to Do?"

A few hundred of us have gathered to share our personal responses to that question, to share resources with one another and to make a long-term commitment to contribute to the end of race-based hatred and violence.

What can we do to educate ourselves individually and take a stand for fairness and equality?

What can we do to stop the cycle of race-based hatred and violence in our communities?

What do we do to make our companies examples of respectful work environments?

> *"We cannot live for ourselves alone. Our lives are connected by a thousand invisible threads, and along these sympathetic fibres, our actions run as causes and return to us as results."*
>
> Herman Melville

We are also posting our ideas and commitments to other social media sites followed by the hashtag: #MineToDo. It's time for you to make a positive difference

15

doing whatever you can, wherever you are, with the people you come into contact with.

We believe that everyone is not required to be an activist or a politician or an elected official. There are many things any of us can do and actions all of us can take to make a positive difference in our community, our workplace, our school or our city. And it is that collective action that changes the world into a place we all want to live.

If you'd like to join us, visit: www.WhatIsMineToDo.com or you can search within Facebook for the "What Is Mine to Do" group.

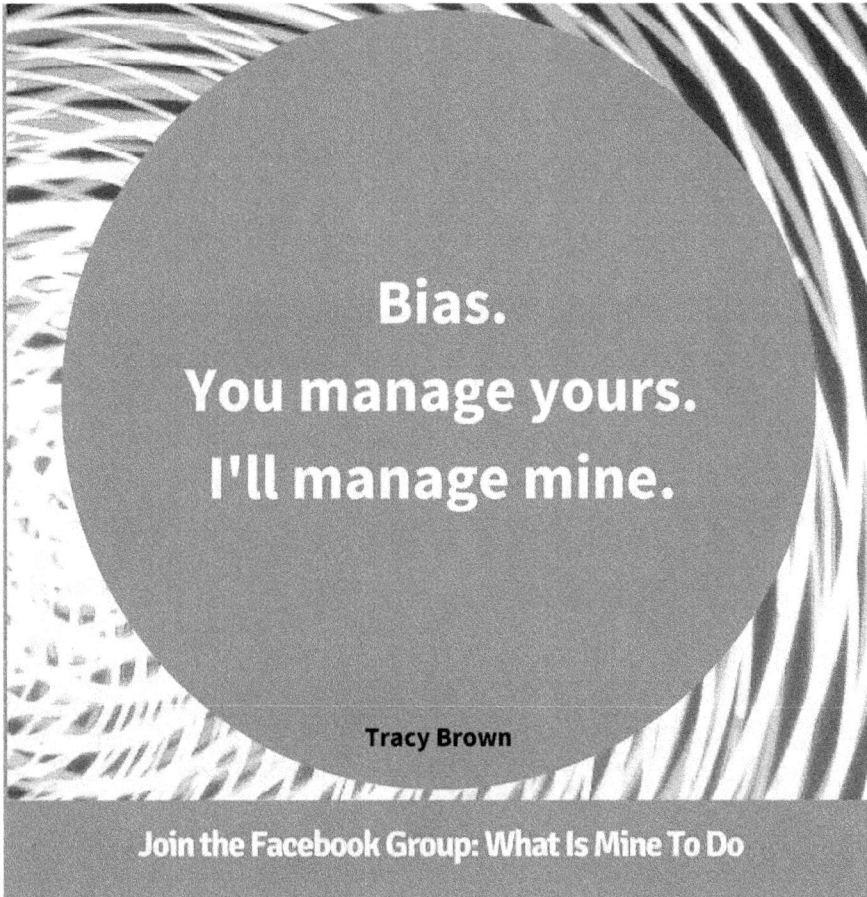

Bias.
You manage yours.
I'll manage mine.

Tracy Brown

Join the Facebook Group: What Is Mine To Do

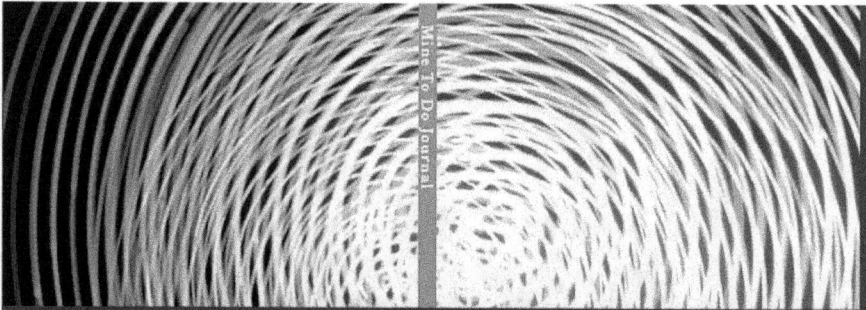

Mine To Do Journal

Tips for Allies

inspire hope.
encourage authenticity.
create a safe space.
work on building trust.

Tracy Brown

Join the Facebook Group: What Is Mine To Do

Charleston is Not Ferguson

A friend emailed me:

> You know, a lot is being discussed about the
> shooting - race relations, mental illness, hatred, gun
> control. But what has moved me is the way
> Charlestonians are reacting, unlike Baltimore or
> Ferguson. Peaceful, prayerful, forgiving, thoughtful,
> community gatherings, multiple races and
> religions. They are modeling behavior and maybe
> this time some real good will ensue from the tragic
> and horrific event.

While I was not at all surprised by the violent reactions in
Ferguson, Baltimore and around the country, I actually
would have been shocked if there had been riots or a
violent mass community reaction in Charleston.

One major difference is the Charleston event happened in
an historic black church that has been the home to
generation after generation of community leaders in a
stable community. The perpetrator was a stranger to the
community and was not perceived to be a threat. Most
other recently publicized events (i.e. Baltimore, Ferguson
and so many others) happened on the streets in a
community that had an already volatile relationship with
the perpetrator (especially when individual officers are
representatives of an entire police force).

In Charleston, every person in a key leadership
role focused his or her initial comments on the
"victims." In many of the other incidents people who were
in leadership roles initially came to the defense of the

19

perpetrators and discounted any consideration that the person charged or killed might have been charged or killed by mistake. In some cases, within hours or days of the incident there was suspicion of tampering with evidence, covering up the truth or adjusting the information shared with the victims' families and with the public.

There was no element in Charleston of the shooter representing a group that is supposed to protect and serve the very community it has been disrespecting and/or disregarding for a long time. This element of betrayal: by the individual officer, the police force as a whole, elected officials and "the establishment" is not a direct factor in the Charleston tragedy.

Even though the race-hatred in the Charleston case is actually an even bigger betrayal by an entire society, it makes perfect sense that the murders would create sadness and disbelief, but not violence. Other incidents had, in addition to sadness and disbelief, the added element of the majority of the population feeling trapped, caged and tormented by the perpetrator (the police force as an entity) in a scenario that has played out countless times without punishment.

Eggs and Soda

Have you ever left eggs boiling on your stove too long and then you rush to the kitchen when you hear the loud pop of the eggs exploding? All the water has boiled out, the pan is dry and the now burnt eggs have no other option than to crack out of their shell with a loud bang leaving the horrible, lingering smell of burnt food. That would be Ferguson.

On the other hand, have you ever opened a can of soda with a pop top? It's something you've done many times and there's never been a problem before. But imagine that today you grab the can of soda that's been bumping around in the back of your car on your drive from the store to your destination, and without thinking you pop the top. It fizzes, the soda explodes out of the can and you have a major, sticky mess all over you. This shock and surprise is Charleston: a messy surprise without any directly related precipitating element of boiling over or burning out.

Pain, Sorrow and Forgiveness

Don't misunderstand me. I don't mean to downplay the deep pain and sorrow from the loss of 9 innocent lives. Nine people were killed for no good reason. It is truly devastating; not only to the family members and church members of the deceased but to all caring people in the world. In addition, this particular loss pulls the scab off a never healed wound for African Americans.

- Black people nationwide are in mourning. Too many of us were alive when four little girls were killed in a church in Birmingham Alabama. We see history repeating itself in ways we believed could never happen again.

- Black people nationwide are angry, for it is inexcusable that our nation continues to allow the negative stereotypes and race-based hatred to continue with little consequence.

21

- Black people nationwide are afraid. Stereotypes and racial profiling make it difficult to feel safe in any situation.

- Black people nationwide are, once again, in forgiveness mode: it is something we know too well how to do. Some might argue that no group of people in this country has had more to forgive.

But the idea that the prayer and forgiveness demonstrated in Charleston is a model from which *"some real good"* will come is a dangerous statement.

Now, before I go on, let me interject that the friend who used that phrase is someone I know well enough to know that what I am about to say does not apply to her. But reading it made me realize how many times in the last 24 hours I had heard or read white people saying how impressed they are at how peaceful, loving or forgiving "those poor people in Charleston" are.

- The inference that black people, in pain, should not be violent even after years, decades or centuries of mistreatment is ridiculous. Some real good should come from us, as a nation, waking up to demand no one in any community should ever feel that kind of pain again.

- The implication that "the norm" is for black people to react with violence or anger is a slippery slope. Believing that makes it okay for police to wear riot gear, bring in military equipment and raise the tension level with threatening tactics when there is a situation in the black community. But when faced with hundreds of bikers with guns and actual

22

deaths, those arrested were trusted to sit without handcuffs, using their cell phones and having conversation. Considering the thousands, if not millions, of incidents that occur in the course of a year involving black people in the U.S. the number that turn violent is a tiny percentage. Some real good should come from us realizing anger and violence is an exception, not the norm.

- Since there is a publicly acknowledged pattern of black teenagers being roughly handled, assumed dangerous or considered such a threat that they are injured or killed primarily because of a mental profile that exists in a peace officer's head, some real good should come from us seeing the lie.

- When white people just feel safer because black people in pain are praying and forgiving instead of protesting or rioting, then they are missing the point. Black people forgiving white people is nothing new; Black people have earned a few dozen PhD degrees in forgiving white people. Black people forgiving white people is not a difficult assignment. I can't speak for all black people but I would venture to say a whole lot of black people would love it if instead of praising us for being forgiving, white people would engage in ongoing action that made it no longer necessary to forgive white people for race-based hate. That would be some real good.

I am not an advocate for violent protests or riots. But I do know that people who are angry in reaction to horrific conditions are the people who most need to be listened to, partnered with and given a voice. The hardest times,

23

and the most challenging situations, might birth the most meaningful and long-lasting changes. So, as long as we only come to the table with people who don't threaten us and who make us feel safe we'll keep excusing ourselves from making real, deep, substantive change.

Black people praying and forgiving won't fix our society's quickness to label the white shooter mentally ill instead of a criminal, a terrorist or some other descriptor that fits. If we say the shooter in Charleston was mentally ill, do we believe the shooter in Ferguson was also mentally ill? Were the police officers in Baltimore mentally ill? Was Trayvon Martin's killer mentally ill? Were the young men who put a noose around the neck of James Byrd and dragged him from the back of their truck mentally ill? Has every white person who arrested or killed or dragged or tormented a black person because of race-based stereotypes mentally ill?

Whether you answered yes or no you have to consider this: if any of these people is excused for their actions because they are deemed mentally ill, then we must follow that thought and recognize that the pervasive pattern of these kinds of incidents then logically indicates that the United States of America is certifiably mentally ill. Maybe we, as a collective nation, need to be in therapy. Are you willing to have that conversation?

In the bigger picture, it's really not practical (or fair) to compare the Charleston experience to the experience in Baltimore, Ferguson or any other place. That would be like comparing the strategies and tactics of Martin Luther King Jr and Malcolm X in order to name one more important or more valuable than the other. We needed

24

BOTH of these men and both of their approaches to effect meaningful and long-lasting change. They created a necessary tension in ideology which allowed for a range of options for action. Neither one was completely peaceful. Neither was completely violent. Both were guided by a spiritually based philosophy and a deep love for unity, equity and respect.

We don't all need to agree on all the tactics but we do need to agree - and commit to - our target destination: a country where race-based hatred and race-based violence is not acceptable.

The time for sleeping has ended. The alarm clock has been ringing for a while and it's time to stop hitting the snooze button. We are about to be late to work for the umpteenth time and if we don't change this pattern soon we may be put on final probation.

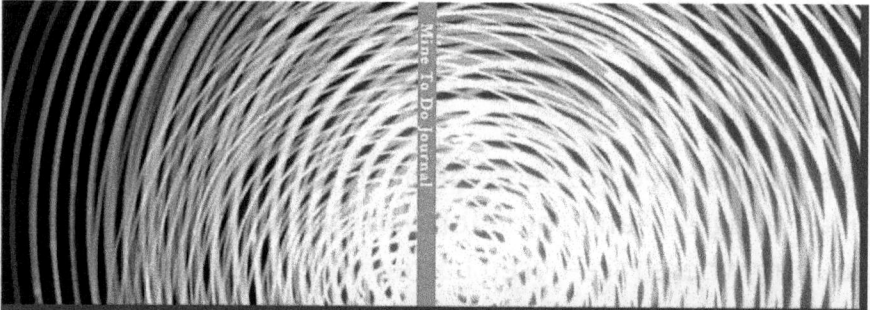

Mine To Do Journal

Tips for Allies

inspire a new perspective.
encourage new behaviors.
create a way from no way.
work to make a difference.

Tracy Brown

Join the Facebook Group: What Is Mine To Do

Ferguson: Talk About It

I don't think many people are surprised that Darren Wilson, the police officer who shot and killed 18-year old Michael Brown was not indicted by the Grand Jury. Don't get me wrong; there were probably many people who were hoping for a different outcome. But hoping is not the same as expecting. So after St. Louis County Prosecutor Robert McCulloch made his very long and very detailed announcement that the grand jury had voted "No True Bill" on all five counts, most of the follow up commentary was focused on encouraging peaceful protest and nonviolent action.

In his remarks after the decision was announced, President Obama said, "This is an issue for America, not just Ferguson." And I want to add, "This is an issue for the workplace, not just the courtroom."

Historically, managers and supervisors would say the taboo topics to discuss at work included religion, politics and sex. Did that ever stop employees from talking about these topics? Of course not! And now, with everyone having all the news of the world in the palm of their hands (via smart phones, tablets and other technology) it is absolutely ridiculous to think employees will ignore the hottest news of the day.

I am telling my clients to intentionally talk about this Michael Brown / Darren Wilson case. Used in an intentional way, these kinds of conversations are an excellent way to bring relevance to an organization's commitment to diversity and inclusion. Most people don't like to participate in role plays during training because it

27

feels forced and fake. These same people are often easy to engage when asked to relate a current "hot topic" in the news to their own community or workplace.

Some Questions to Encourage Healthy, Helpful Dialogue about the Ferguson Case & the Grand Jury Decision

- What do you think it's like to feel invisible, excluded or judged? Are there groups in our organization that feel their contribution is not valued?

- Are there different identity groups within our organization that tend to be stereotyped in negative ways (think beyond race and ethnicity; often this happens based on job function, department location or some other distinction.) How does this affect productivity (or teamwork, quality, safety)?

- Do we have any customers who might be feeling unsafe or unsupported as a result of the grand jury decision? How might this affect our customer service and sales interactions?

- Are there any leaders (or teams) that are perceived as so powerful and intimidating that they are feared and avoided?

- When employees in our company feel stifled or mistreated, do you think they are aware of ways to receive support ... or do they believe their only recourse is to cause trouble, file a lawsuit or behave badly?

28

- Are there employees in our workforce who have a desire to get involved in our own community to address the tension between police officers and certain neighborhoods? (The millennial generation is often very concerned about community service and making a positive difference. Is this an opportunity to initiate a community service project or partnership?)

Using the Ferguson case in a deliberate way helps employees experience the difference between dialogue and debate.

Debate would focus on whether you agree or disagree with the grand jury decision.

Dialogue would focus on how aspects of the case might relate to behaviors, systems or cultural norms in your organization.

Dialogue also makes it safe for people to share how this case affects them personally and for other employees to get a perspective different from their own.

So don't be so quick to avoid or shut down the conversation. And don't rush to take sides or look for who is right and who is wrong. Instead, use dialogue inspired by this current event to uncover both hidden biases and hidden opportunities in your organization.

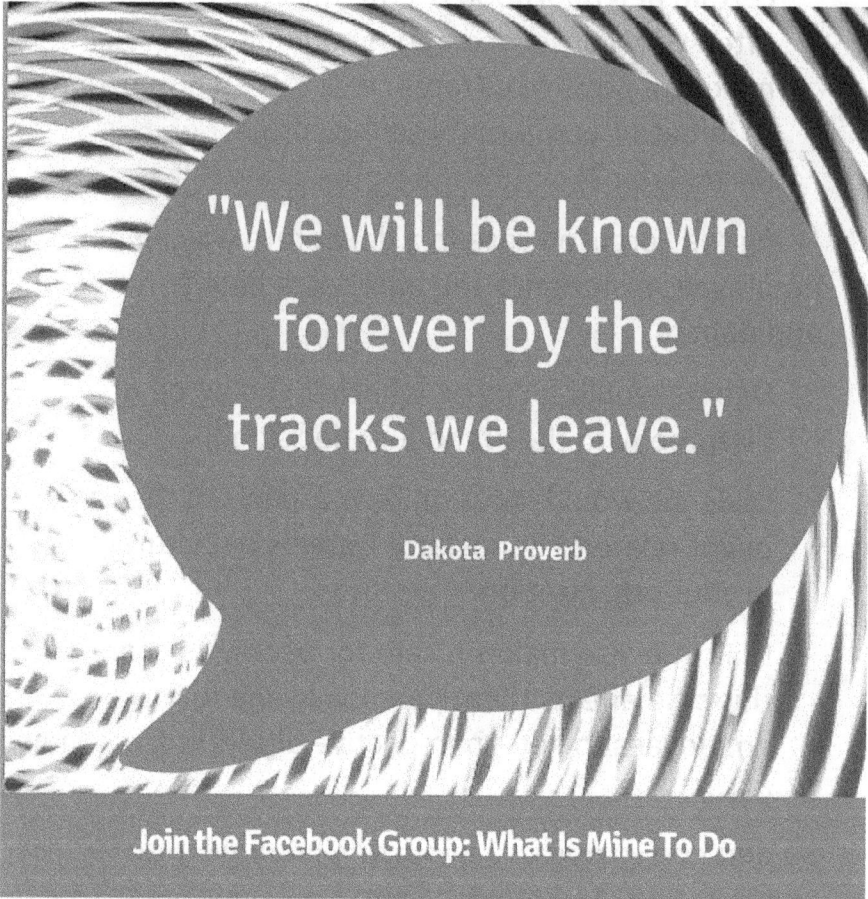

"We will be known forever by the tracks we leave."

Dakota Proverb

Join the Facebook Group: What Is Mine To Do

30

Afraid to Talk about Race?

Does it feel like you are walking on eggshells whenever the conversation turns to the subject of racial identity, race relations or racism? In the last few weeks people have said these comments to me:

1. "I'm afraid if I say the wrong thing, I'll be judged and humiliated."

2. "I'd like to get to know some of my co-workers (of a different race) better but I just don't feel comfortable going up to them and starting a conversation. It's awkward."

3. "Talking about race gets everybody all upset and emotional. So I just avoid the subject."

4. "Well, they always flock together at lunch time and at breaks so I figured they just didn't want me to participate with them."

5. "I'm bi-racial so I hate it when it feels like people are putting pressure on me to take sides."

6. "Why even talk about race? It's just man-made foolishness anyway. I treat everybody the same."

What if you could talk about race in a way that helped you communicate better with people you work? What if you could talk about race in a way that helped you understand people in your community better? What if you could talk about race in a way that gave you deeper insights into your own cultural background, beliefs and baggage?

I've helped thousands of people release their fear of talking about race. I've guided people through processes that supported healthy dialogue about racial identity and the impact of race relations on all of us. And I've reminded people that even though racial identity is only one of the ways we might be different from each other, it is a differentiation that has been interwoven with just about every aspect of American culture.

Five Discussion Starters

I'll share five questions you can use to solicit a deeper level of conversation about the impact of race on the lives of people you know.

1. When you were a child, what did you learn about racism?

2. How do you feel when race-based violence is featured in the news?

3. What feels important to you about race relations in our city or company?

4. I've decided to take a stand for respect and positive race relations. What suggestions do you have for me?

5. What advice would you give teens today about race, racism or race relations?

These are just a few of the questions you can use to encourage people to share more about their own perspectives related to race. Just remember, you are asking them to tell you about their personal experience or perception so there are no answers that are wrong and no responses that are better or worse. If you ask these questions you have to do your part and listen without judgment and without comparing their response to your own.

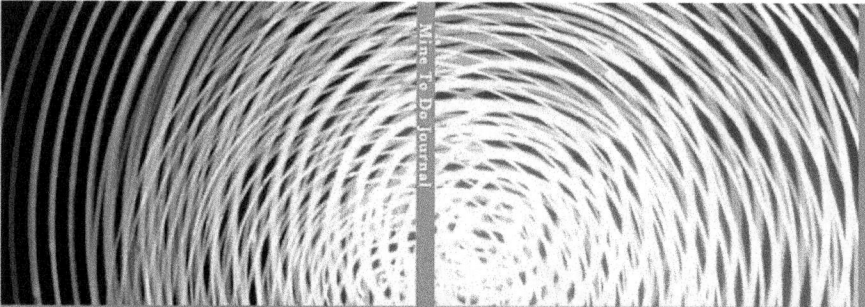

Listen
for understanding,
not agreement.

Tracy Brown

Join the Facebook Group: What Is Mine To Do

The More Things Change, the More They Stay the Same

My parents bought a 3 story home with full basement and large front and back yards on a tree-lined street in the West End of St Louis when I was 2 years old. There was a long driveway the length of the property. My mother had rose bushes and grew vegetables in the back yard. There were good schools in walking distance and a library I loved just a few blocks away.

My parents worked hard to afford this home, this neighborhood and to ensure their five children had food, received a good education, participated in church, took music or dance classes, went to summer camp, and were involved in extracurricular activities.

But according to a flyer widely distributed back then, my parents were Negroes who had INVADED that part of the city! And apparently other hard working, family oriented people just like them were about to stage a "take over" on the south side of the city in the early-to-mid 60's.

Does anyone else find it ironic that immigrants (mostly German and Italian) would consider themselves more American than African Americans who had been in the U.S. longer? Or that immigrants would be scaling an all-out effort to protect themselves from a population of African Americans who were born in the United States?

ATTENTION: VOTERS, Tax Payers, Property Owners & Business People. A Special Organizing Meeting at the Jefferson Saving & Loan at Cherokee & California AUG. 27th at 7:30 P. M.

A number of things will be Discussed at this Meeting, The Purpose of this Organization will be made known.

There will be a Landlord who will tell you of his Experience with Negro Tennants this should be of great Interest and Value to every Property Owner or Rental Property, Especially since the Passage of the Cival Rights Bill.

The Cival Rights Bill Requires you to Sell and Rent your Property to Negroes, to Employ them, to Serve them in your Resturants, Taverns, Hotels etc. and under certain conditions to rent to them to live in your own Home.

The more you Know about Negroes the better you can handle and deal with them.

The Negroes have already Invaded the Central Part, the North and West Parts of the City and Now they are Threatening to Invade the South Part of the City Especially in the German Neighborhoods etc.

Be sure to attend this Important Meeting and bring your Friends Lets Organize the Negro is already Organized and Many are Armed!

St. Louis Property Owners of America, P.O. Box 9142, Richmond Heights, Mo. 631 nd Council of Voters and all Affiliated Organizations.

Is this what some people call, playing the "race" card? I don't share this for pity. I don't share this to cause white people to feel guilty. It's more fascinating than frustrating.

Actually, what strikes me first is how so many people refer to this time in our history as if it were 500 or 5,000 years ago instead of 50 years ago. I can't count the number of times people in workshops or seminars think of these attitudes and actions as so distant and so different from America today. Every time that happens I quietly think to myself, "Wait. This all happened in MY lifetime. This happened to me ... and my family."

And way too often, the person making these kinds of comments was a child during the 50s or 60s and I think, "Wait. This was all happening during YOUR childhood; why are you acting like you don't know about it?"

And with younger adults, I want to look in their eyes and say, "Your parents grew up with this; go have a conversation with them!" But then I realize that if their parents had anything helpful to say about it, these younger people would have already heard it and wouldn't be making the uninformed comments they were making.

The second thing that strikes me is how the justification given to treat black people unfairly, and the rationale used to explain why people of one group are not equal to another group, really hasn't changed all that much. The group being excluded might be different but the rhetoric is all too familiar.

The third thing that strikes me is the irony of using the phrase "It is the Constitutional Right of all Americans" (a) to lead into a list of 'rights' I've never noticed in the U.S. Constitution and (b) to defend excluding a group of people who are Americans too.

I might be totally off-base but it seems to me there are political activists and media celebrities in the 21st century who have continued to use a very similar approach to justify exclusionary behavior, discriminatory policies or judgmental positions. Sometimes it feels like "the more things change, the more they stay the same."

37

IS THE CIVIL RIGHTS LAW RIGHT?

It violates the THIRTEENTH AMENDMENT, which prohibits Involuntary service and slavery.

It violates the FOURTH and TENTH AMENDMENTS which limit Federal power.

It is the Constitutional Right of every American:

1, To choose customers.
2. To choose associates.
3. To choose the environment in which to raise a family.
4. To choose a neighborhood.
5. To choose employees.
6. To post signs at a place of business stating the policy of service.
7. To equal rights to all and without special priviliges --- REGARDLESS OF RACE.

FREEDOM OF CHOICE MUST BE PROTECTED --- OTHERWISE FREEDOM WILL VANISH. FREEDOM OF CHOICE IS THE BEDROCK UPON WHICH ALL FREEDOMS REST.

Allowing black people to live anywhere they could afford to live; or to work in any job they were qualified to fill, apparently was giving them "special priviliges" (sp) that took away the right (for someone who was white) to have a good life. Really?

And the fourth thing that stands out to me is how many typos and grammatical errors I seem to find in not only these flyers but in many documents that are used to convince one group that another group is going to lower their quality of life and bring their neighborhood, school or workplace standards down.

38

or service.

7. To equal rights to all and without special priviliges --- REGARDLESS OF RACE.

FREEDOM OF CHOICE MUST BE PROTECTED --- OTHERWISE FREEDOM WILL VANISH. FREEDOM OF CHOICE IS THE BEDROCK UPON WHICH ALL FREEDOMS REST.

The word ACCOMMODATION is used to mean involuntary servitude - forced service - slavery. Thousands of young Americans died to put an end to this in the Civil war of the 1860s.

VOTE AGAINST any candidate who supports PUBLIC ACCOMMODATION or CIVIL RIGHTS.

FREE AMERICA AND EVERY AMERICAN'S RIGHT OF PRIVATE PROPERTY MUST BE PRESERVED.

Mob Law encouragement (Anarchy) by faulty Court decisions Legislation and Politics leads to chaos. State and National sovereignty must be preserved.

St. Louis Property Owners Association of America   P.O. Box 9142
Richmond Heights, Missouri 63117

Organizations please copy and circulate as widely as possible, millions of copies.

But I do find it amusing that the flyer above ends with: "Organizations please copy and circulate as widely as possible, millions of copies." It's funny to me because in today's world, with today's technology, reaching millions of people can happen in a few seconds. Back then it required paper and printing and planning and postage fees. But it also is funny when you consider this: in 1960, even though St Louis was the 10th largest city in the U.S. it only had a population of just over 750,000 people. Now, think about it. If a portion of that number were children, and a portion of that number were those notorious, invading Negroes, and a significant portion of the population was living in those parts of town that had already been hopelessly invaded, why were "millions" of copies needed?

It's not clear to me whether these flyers were in reaction to the Civil Rights Act of 1957, 1964 or 1966. But they sure helped me better understand the mentality of the protesters who daily greeted my bus full of dangerous little 4th graders during my first month or two of that school year. The school I was sent to was south of Forest Park and Interstate 40, so even though it was not located in the most threatening parts of south St Louis it was in an area that could be considered the unofficial entrance to the south side of St. Louis. No wonder protesters carried signs, called us names and threatened us and the school board in an attempt to ensure there would be no Negro children invading any schools further south any time soon.

As you might expect, The St Louis Property Owners Association of America (that created the flyers above) no longer exists. And you won't easily find these documents, or others like them, on the internet because very few organizations would be proud to display them in this day and age. The flyers come from a private collection; my aunt somehow knew this was history to be saved.

But then, that shouldn't surprise me. She was the first black nurse hired to work at the Veteran's Hospital in St Louis. Through an unplanned series of 'mishaps' they didn't realize she was black until after she had been hired

40

... and even though it was a government funded hospital there was much drama to be had. But that's another story for another day.

For now, I just want to remind you if we, as a nation, want to end race-based hatred and violence we must:

- stop denying its existence
- stop pretending it only affects a tiny percentage of the population
- stop accusing the victims
- stop blaming politicians and
- stop waiting for someone else to take action

Instead ask yourself this question: WHAT IS MINE TO DO? Then get busy building positive, proactive relationships in your community and start making a positive difference in your part of the world.

"If you dig a pit for me, you dig one for yourself."

American Indian - Creole

Join the Facebook Group: What Is Mine To Do

Racism Exists: Don't Let It Define You

If you are a person of color in the United States, you have probably heard many white people deny that racism exists. You've been blamed for seeing a problem where there is none. You've been accused of using "the race card" when all you were doing was sharing an actual experience you've had. You've been told my people in authority positions to just not talk about it.

RACISM exists. It is not your imagination. But once you realize that, what can you do about it? How do you keep racism from ruining your career – or your self-esteem?

Racism -- or any other ism -- results from the combination of prejudice with power. But all racism is not the same.

Different Types of Racism

Institutional racism shows up in the systematic denial of services or opportunities based on race. Obviously this is the level where company policies, community access to business development, or societal standards of beauty are affected.

Individual racism is evident when individuals treat other people or groups unfairly, using race as the determining factor.

Unaware racism is the most common kind. This occurs when the impact of decisions or actions result in negative consequences, but the person or organization was not intentionally targeting a negative outcome.

43

Obviously, unaware or unintentional racism often occurs because people are not conscious and aware of their prejudices. Prejudice means, "to prejudge" and we all have prejudices.

Comments and actions we often label as "racist" reflect the existence of institutional racism in our society. But many individuals don't realize that what they are saying or doing could be interpreted as racist because their behavior reflects what they've heard others say or what they've seen others do.

The big challenge with all racism, whether it is intentional or not, is that it has a negative effect on individuals who are part of the ostracized or stereotyped group.

Racism creates "outsiders" and "insiders" based on race or ethnicity instead of inclusion being based on skills, talents, values and experience.

Internalized Oppression

A dangerous side effect of racism is a condition known as internalized oppression. Internalized oppression is a term used to describe ways members of a group hold themselves back.

For example, as people of color we might anticipate a negative response based on our race, so we don't even try. Or we believe "the hype" or the historical myth about what the dominant group will allow, so we don't go after what we really want.

How many times have you heard someone say, "I'm not going to apply for that job. You know they don't hire 'us' in that department." Or, "I'm not going to the company picnic. They don't want us there anyway."

Those are examples of internalized oppression. We limit ourselves without any limiting actions being initiated or enforced by the mainstream.

The other way internalized oppression hurts us in the workplace or in our community is when we believe opportunities for people in our group are limited. As a result, we focus on competing with others in our group, rather than supporting each other.

If you think there's only one spot for an African American manager in your business unit and you want that spot . . . then it's easy for you to justify withholding important information or saying negative things about someone else who might be considered your competition.

Internalized oppression leads us to hurt ourselves, and others in our identity group, by applying self-imposed limitations.

Success Strategies

If you are a person of color, there are many things you can do to experience success and keep moving on the fast track — even when racism exists.

See people as individuals. Just like you don't want people to judge you based on their assumptions about all blacks or all minorities or all men . . . eliminate your tendency to stereotype others.

Choose your battles. You don't need to respond every time someone does or says something you might consider racist. If you believe the person was intentionally offensive, and the effect of their actions is harmful to your career (not just your ego) then you should confront. If there is a policy or program which consistently discriminates, you should challenge it.

But if the action appears to be unintentional, you might consider whether this is worth confronting at this time.

Or, if the person is someone you don't interact with on a regular basis you might choose to ignore the comment or behavior completely.

Focus your confrontations on people you need to have ongoing relationships with or policies that directly affect your success.

Learn to confront in a positive manner. Develop the skills to confront the situation or challenge the behavior without labeling the other person a racist. Otherwise, they will become defensive and no progress will be made. Your goal should be to (a) educate them or (b) change the behavior.

If your goal is to hurt them or get revenge, you may win the short-term battle but you'll lose the long-term war of building a successful career or achieving your shared goals and objectives.

Get involved. The more people in your workplace feel like they know you, the more you will benefit. No one progresses based on skills or commitment alone. You have to have a multicultural group of allies who know your experience and talents. Get involved in activities or projects you have an interest in. You'll meet people with common interests and expand your network at the same time.

Participate in professional associations. Professional associations will help you understand the industry, the company and the type of work you do from a larger perspective. This will help you build a career beyond your current job. It will also give you a broader network of people who are familiar with your skills and talents.

Stay focused on your goals. Keep racism from ruining your career by setting clear goals and developing a plan to achieve those goals. Instead of focusing on all the barriers resulting from racism, find the people in your organization who can help you move forward.

Responsibility and Action

Racism does exist in our society and in the organizations in which we work. But that's not a good enough excuse to short-circuit your career.

We come from a long history of leaders who achieved in spite of racism. You can do the same!

Tips for Allies

inspire by your actions.

encourage risk taking.

create options.

work on yourself.

Tracy Brown

Join the Facebook Group: What Is Mine To Do

Are Black People Killing Cops to Get Revenge?

Navigating the impact of race in our complex world isn't easy. There are many layers of the onion we have to pull back to get to the real issues or the hidden beliefs that might be contributing to the events we are experiencing.

And it is especially complicated talking about the group experience while still respecting that each of us is an individual. Any conversation about "white people" and "black people" has to be navigated considering both group patterns and individual behavior at the same time. A pattern that applies to the whole often doesn't reflect the beliefs or behaviors of a specific person.

People of color in general, and black people specifically, are accustomed to navigating this because they are often referred to or judged as a group. White people in America are still generally uncomfortable or unaware of themselves as both part of a group norm and an individual who has beliefs and behaviors different from that norm.

In the last 2 days I have had 3 people talk to me directly about this alleged "war on cops" that has been declared to get even for all the black men and women killed by police officers. Two of the three I talked with shared an observation that no one seems concerned about police officers being killed. One asked me point blank, "Do you think black people are killing cops to get revenge?"

The short answer is, "No."

Are there any individuals, who are black, who have decided to hurt or kill a police officer just because he is an officer? Yes.

But when Dylann Roof invited himself to attend Bible Study at Emanuel A.M.E. Church and killed 9 black people just because they were black there was no assumption that white people, in general, were declaring war on black people. No one assumed his actions were an indicator that we should prepare for all young, white men to kill black people in churches across America. Even when fires were set in a dozen black churches during the weeks after the Charleston murders, no one assumed white people overall were now feeling empowered or encouraged to set black churches on fire nationwide.

Yet, when a few black individuals attack or kill white police officers, there is a rush to apply collective blame and incite collective fear.

When these few isolated incidents have occurred I've observed huge support for police officers. This makes me happy. Being a peace officer is an important and dangerous job. But there is a difference between officers being killed in the line of duty and officers being targeted just because they are in uniform. It seems like almost every officer death recently is being lumped into one bucket and tied to race, which isn't true.

Scanning the news and social media I haven't picked up on any trend of any group expressing the attitude of "that cop had it coming." There is no pattern of groups organizing and encouraging individuals to go out and shoot police officers. Although I will admit I have heard this assumption (that we should expect many more officers will be killed by black people getting revenge) espoused by a few individual commentators using their own analysis or opinion as their source.

Actually, what I've seen more of is this: After acknowledging the wrong of any officer being ambushed or targeted simply because of the uniform, the commentary has most often observed how quickly "the public" has become upset about a few officers while still being in denial or apathy about the hundreds of black people killed by police each year and the hundreds of thousands of people of color harassed by police or treated unfairly within the justice system. Some bloggers have noticed that many who are saying, "There's a war on cops!" never have expressed concerned about the demonstrated war on black people.

Of course, typically none of us care about people we don't relate to or feel connected to in a personal way. So this "war on cops" reaction makes it even more obvious that in our current society (most) white people feel connected to the role of the police officer (regardless of color) but do not feel related to, or connected to, the daily experience of (most) people of color.

The logic that "Black people must be killing cops to give them what they deserve" is the same logic that leads to

51

believing - in spite of documented evidence otherwise - "More black people get killed by cops because they are the ones committing the crimes. They just are getting what *they* deserve."

But what we know is this:

No one deserves to be killed just because of the color of their skin, the color of their uniform, their sexual orientation, their religion or ANY group identity they are a part of.

And the other thing we know - or should know by now - is that, as a group, black people in this nation have never been driven or guided by revenge. If revenge were the motivation, there would already be a whole lot of dead white people lining every street in the nation. And beyond killing white people, what would revenge for decades of slavery, Jim Crow laws, employment discrimination, health care discrimination and more even look like?

- When Ken Chenault became CEO of American Express he would have fired all the white people to get even for all the jobs black people were denied for centuries.

- When cities elected black mayors they would have made sure the black neighborhoods had superior service and response times leaving white neighborhoods to wait or worry about their needs.

- Or when black managers were promoted to leadership positions they might have only hired black people because that's what white people in leadership had done in the past (i.e. hire their own and deny others).

- When a black doctor received his medical degree he would only save the lives of black people and let white people die.

- Or a black teacher would earmark every white student in her class as slow or see them as a discipline problem.

This idea that black people want revenge and will behave the way white people have behaved is not only ridiculous but also a dangerous false belief that breeds distrust and builds subconscious barriers.

The message more often heard in black communities is: "We're not trying to be like white people. White people are the ones who have put all this inequity and hatred in place. We never want to use their logic or treat whole groups of people the way they have treated us."

Black people don't want revenge. Black people want respect.

So don't get caught up in the hype. Don't be fooled by the rhetoric. Avoid people who are trying to incite distrust, anger, resentment or fear. Stay connected with people you know to be focused on equity, dignity, partnership and collaboration.

We all need that. Both individually and collectively.

"True peace is not merely the absence of tension; it is the presence of justice."

Martin Luther King Jr

Join the Facebook Group: What Is Mine To Do

54

Privilege and Personal Responsibility

Everyone understands the dictionary definition of the word privilege. It refers to extras, bonuses or gifts provided to recognize someone's position or achievement.

Merriam-Webster Dictionary defines privilege as: a special right, advantage, or immunity granted or available only to a particular person or group of people

---

So it can be confusing when you hear the term "white privilege" or "male privilege" because, in that context, it is actually referring to *unearned* benefits. Privilege, in this context, is referring to the unsolicited and automatic ways cultural norms support and empower a dominant or designated group. Like so many words in the English language you have to know the context to understand the meaning.

Earned Privilege versus Unearned Privilege

Most of us have both earned privilege and unearned privilege. We feel entitled to those privileges we have earned. But unless we are careful observers, or pay attention to feedback from others, we can be completely unaware of the unearned privileges we enjoy.

I am a black woman and I have both earned and unearned privilege. I have earned the benefits I receive based on

55

working hard and getting a college degree. I have earned the respect I receive based on my achievements in the world of business.

But I also have unearned benefits as someone who is "able-bodied" and doesn't have to think about any extra steps or requirements that might be needed to navigate through my busy week using a wheelchair or relying on a sign-language interpreter.

I am responsible for the earned privileges. I actually am not responsible for the unearned privileges, but once I am aware of them I can behave responsibly to ensure these unearned benefits do not give me an unfair advantage.

The Biggest Indication of White Privilege

The biggest indicator of white privilege is the choice to ignore the negative impact of racial disparity in the daily lives of everyone else.

Some might say it's hard to notice what you don't experience. However, what I hear over and over from white people nationwide is that they recognize others are treated unfairly based primarily on the color of their skin but

- they don't know what to do about it, or
- they don't want to make waves, or
- they don't want to get in a big debate with their family or coworkers, or
- they are simply afraid to say the wrong thing so they don't say anything.

Say or Do Something

But it is important to say or do something.

Martin Luther King, Jr said, "In the end, we will remember not the words of our enemies, but the silence of our friends."

At TEDxSMU I shared that one of the biggest shifts that has been occurring since the Charleston murders in June 2015 has been the large numbers of white people calling out the disrespectful, discriminatory and damaging behavior of other white people.

This is a trend worth noting, for it has always required the active engagement of people from all groups to effect a long-lasting improvement in conflict situations.

We know that legislation alone doesn't guarantee respect or equity. It is our individual behavior with the people we come into contact with, in the places we live, work and worship that actually define what is acceptable - and what is unacceptable - in our local and national culture.

> *"Neither policy nor position can block the passion of inspired and committed people."*
> Tracy Brown

Are You Inspired and Committed?

So I encourage you, if you want to create a world that demonstrates respect and fairness, find something to do that makes a positive difference.

You don't have to be an activist. You don't have to go on a hunger strike. You don't have to spend your day trying to catch someone in engaging in a blatantly discriminatory

57

act. You don't have to join a new political action group and start organizing your entire town.

All of those things are great options if you are drawn to them. But taking small actions that fit into your daily life are just as important.

- You might initiate a conversation and build a relationship at work with someone from a different ethnic group you've never really talked to before.
- You might include a book written by a person of color in your book club's reading list.
- You could listen with compassion when a person of color shares their pain or frustration and recognize they actually have a different experience than you do.
- You might listen to understand and not expect or require agreement
- You could refuse to laugh (or you could walk away) after a neighbor's racial slur or race-based joke.
- You could notice when someone in a meeting is being overlooked or discounted and either invite their input or affirm their good suggestion.

There are countless things you can do, but most of the time we focus on what we can't do and think our individual action won't make a big difference.

This week, no matter what racial group you identify with, do at least one thing that demonstrates you want to help create a world where race-based violence and hatred are no longer acceptable.

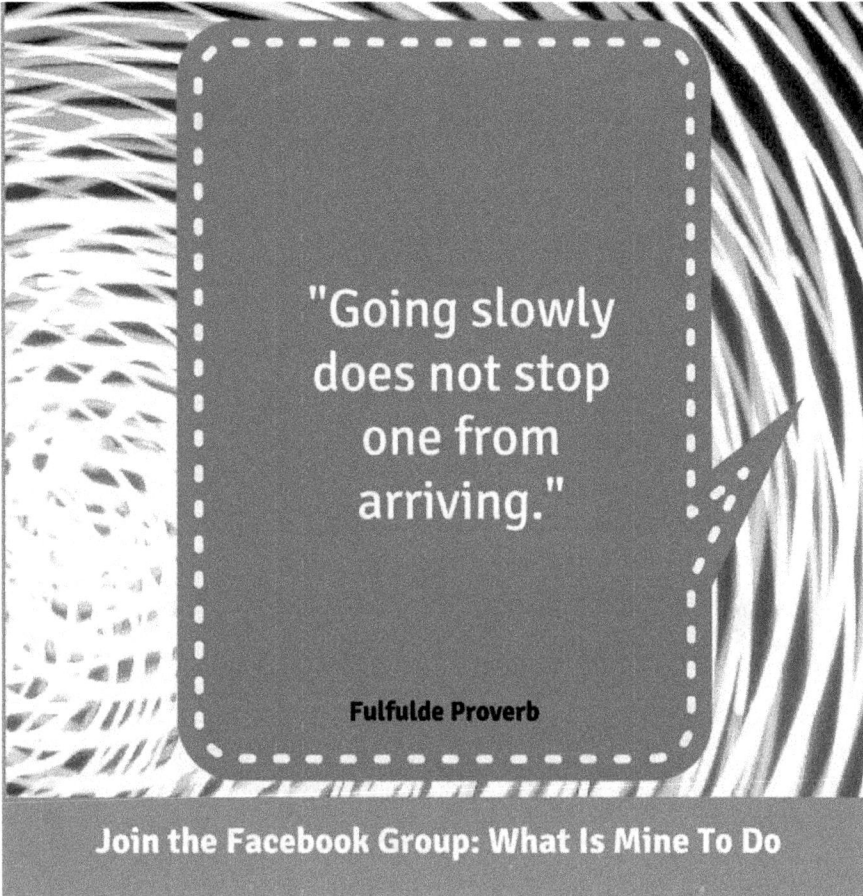

"Going slowly does not stop one from arriving."

Fulfulde Proverb

Join the Facebook Group: What Is Mine To Do

Everyone has biases.
Reinforce the ones you want.
Replace the ones you don't.

Tracy Brown

Join the Facebook Group: What Is Mine To Do

What Does a Neighbor Look Like?

Imagine: You lock yourself out of your home. You call a locksmith. Shortly after you are safe in your home and the locksmith has departed, 19 armed police officers arrive because a neighbor who didn't recognize you reported a residential burglary.

What Does a Thief Look Like?

This is not fiction. It is the unfortunate story of unearned privilege trumping earned privilege. A white man (who made sure it was known that he is an attorney) couldn't imagine that a black woman (who has an MBA and is a Vice President in her corporate job) could be living in his neighborhood.

Fay Wells, the black woman, said:

"It didn't matter that I told the cops I'd lived there for seven months, told them about the locksmith, offered to show a receipt for his services and my ID. It didn't matter that I went to Duke, that I have an MBA from Dartmouth, that I'm a vice president of strategy at a multinational corporation. It didn't matter that I've never had so much as a speeding ticket. It didn't matter that I calmly, continually asked them what was happening."

She continued, "It also didn't matter that I didn't match the description of the person they were looking for — my neighbor described me as Hispanic when he called 911. What mattered was that I was a woman of color trying to get into her apartment — in an almost entirely white apartment complex in a mostly white city — and a white man who lived in another building called the cops because he'd never seen me before."

Safety First, Right?

Who can fault anyone for reporting a suspected burglary? Most of us want to live in neighborhoods where we can count on our neighbors to keep a watchful eye on what's happening for the safety and wellbeing of everyone.

What's critical to notice, however, is who we assume is safe and who we assume is not safe. Think about who you think "looks like" they should be in your neighborhood and who shouldn't.

What's also important to consider is whether the police response was appropriate. There is no question a response from the police was warranted; I wouldn't want the police to refuse to respond if my home was being burglarized. But was the dispatch of 19 officers - who allegedly started with guns pulled and neither asked for nor confirmed identity before taking strong, physical action - either appropriate or necessary?

Maybe I'm naive but I would think any situation like this would begin with asking for identification. Was there some other extenuating circumstance that made the officers believe there might be a gang or group of armed criminals

62

behind the closed door even though the neighbor reported only one person (or possibly two people if he saw the locksmith)? Was there a recent string of burglaries in that neighborhood with a similar description of the suspect? Had there been a pattern of officers being ambushed or shot at when responding to residential burglaries in sunny, Santa Monica, California?

"We don't see things as they are,
we see them as we are."
Anais Nin

You Can Earn Your Way Out of Prejudice

Many people argue that the problems often identified as outcomes of racism aren't racism at all and are actually caused by socio-economic disparities or failure of certain groups to take education seriously or laziness, or some other factor. But the belief that "people of color who get their education and behave responsibly will be viewed and accepted as equals" continues to be proven over and over again as a false belief.

This idea that you can "earn" your way out of prejudice and racism is still more fiction that fact. Fay Wells has undergraduate and graduate degrees from prestigious universities, an executive level position in a multinational company and yet, she looks like a dangerous criminal to a neighbor.

A few months ago on LinkedIn, Bernard Tyson, President and CEO of Kaiser Permanente shared several powerful examples of the way he is treated when he is not in an environment where people know he is the chief executive of a $55 billion company. He said:

63

"You would think my experience as a top executive would be different from a black man who is working in a retail or food service job to support his family."

A couple decades ago, Ellis Cose wrote a powerful book about "The Rage of the Privileged Class." He shared real life stories of black people who were attorneys, corporate executives, successful entrepreneurs and celebrities who were discounted, ignored, threatened and subject to all kinds of negative assumptions that were based on their skin color instead of their skills, experiences or character.

Of course, this is not a new phenomenon. We could go back to the end of slavery and find countless examples. But if we just focus on the so-called "post-Civil Rights" America of the past 25-30 years, I could give you dozens of examples off the top of my head from articles and books on this subject. I could give you hundreds of examples from my own life. But that's not the point.

The point is that the neighbor who made the call may have been so driven by his unearned privilege based on the color of skin, that he didn't even realize he was making a negative assumption about another person based on skin color or race.

The point is that the police response may also have been so driven by assumptions based on skin color that their behavior reflected a "we will do anything we have to do to protect the people of this neighborhood" without consideration that this woman with brown skin also called this neighborhood home.

More recently, in The End of Anger, Ellis Cose examines the current generation of black achievers (people like Fay Wells), their attitudes as well as the decline of white guilt and the inter-generational shifts in how blacks and whites view and interact with each other. It's a much more hopeful book. But the point is that even though so much is better than it has ever been before, it is still far too common for black people to have experiences like Ms. Wells did on a regular basis.

And if these kinds of judgments, stereotypes and assumptions are being made about black people who have achieved educational and career goals that far surpass the average American citizen of any race or color, it's scary to consider the experience of those who are "just average" or those who don't have economic resources to provide greater credibility.

The Neighbor

If Ms. Wells had been a young, white woman waiting for the locksmith would her neighbor have called the police? Or might he have gone out to ask her if she needed some help? We'll never know.

He indicated in his conversation with her that he felt it was Ms. Wells' responsibility to go around and introduce herself to everyone in the neighborhood so they would know she was "ok." But it is obvious he didn't think it was his responsibility to go across the street into another building and make sure all the neighbors there, including Ms. Wells, knew him and knew he was "ok."

65

It's that double standard that's insidious. Unearned privilege shows up as the neighbor's expectation that someone who is different from him must not only (a) recognize what seems "normal" to him but also (b) take on the additional job to actively manipulate the environment in ways that make him feel comfortable, safe or respected.

Where is the neighbor's responsibility to recognize his assumptions, notice his stereotypes or expand his comfort zone? Where is the neighbor's responsibility to apologize for creating such a terrifying and ultimately humiliating experience for this young woman? Where is the neighbor's responsibility to be welcoming and affirming? Where is the neighbor's responsibility to be fair or respectful?

Unfortunately, there is neither reward for the neighbor behaving differently nor is there punishment for him behaving poorly.

> *"If people are good only because they fear punishment, and hope for reward, then we are a sorry lot indeed."*
> Albert Einstein

It makes me wonder if Ms. Wells *had* knocked on his door a few weeks earlier (on a ridiculous quest to meet every neighbor within viewing range of her apartment) might this neighbor have called the police then? Would he have called to report a solicitor who obviously was "casing" the neighborhood preparing to rob everyone? Or might he have assumed he needed to protect his own home and opened the door prepared to shoot an intruder and claim it was self-defense?

That might seem far-fetched to the rational thinker, but what actually happened is equally irrational.

Armchair Quarterback

I am very aware that the article I read was from the viewpoint and experience of Fay Wells with some commentary by the police department.

I am very aware that the neighbor's side of the story isn't shared in this article.

Therefore, I am very aware that most of what I've said about him is speculation or conjecture.

This might seem strange but I actually believe his actions were not intentionally malicious in any way. And I have no desire to judge him personally or demand some action be taken against him. I'd even like to think he did some soul-searching after this incident.

I am simply using this real life story as an example to encourage each one of us to take a closer look at the assumptions we make about people who are different from us in some way. Let's all do the work required to consider ways our assumptions affect the experience others have of feeling welcomed, valued or included in our workplace, neighborhood or spiritual community.

Let's commit to do this work individually and let's commit to do this work collectively, especially as it relates to race, racism and race relations.

Now What?

I prefer to focus on solutions, but there are still so many people I personally know who keep trying to convince me that there really isn't a problem.

> *"It isn't that they can't see the solution. It is that they can't see the problem."*
> Gilbert K. Chesterton

How can this not be a problem?

1. A person with an MBA works as a vice president in her corporate job but, on sight alone, is considered a suspicious & dangerous threat in her own neighborhood.

2. A police force responds with the assumption of guilt and wrong-doing and then, even after they realize she has done nothing wrong, officers continue to disrespect her and refuse to answer her questions.

3. A neighbor is unapologetic for his actions and even rudely dismisses her with profanity.

When this type of event is not an isolated occurrence and is happening on a regular basis in cities nationwide, how can it be ignored? What is it that causes so many white people to be in denial about this?

But more importantly ... what will each one of us do in our own neighborhoods and communities to replace fear with trust, replace pain with partnership and replace ridicule with respect?

"We are all responsible unless we take a stand and speak out against it."

Father Luis Olivares

Join the Facebook Group: What Is Mine To Do

Mine To Do Journal

Give yourself
a learners' permit.

Tracy Brown

Join the Facebook Group: What Is Mine To Do

What Are Your Biases?

Perhaps you've heard others make comments like these:

- "I don't have a prejudiced bone in my body."
- "I am not biased. I treat everyone the same."
- "I'm not prejudiced; I'm a Christian and one of my best friends is Jewish."

If you are saying, "Wait, I really don't have any biases!" then you have failed one of the basic tests for being a champion for diversity and inclusion.

These, and other similar statements, only serve to keep us in denial. When we deny that biases exist we inadvertently give ourselves permission to also ignore our inappropriate behavior. If we believe we have no biases, then anything we do or say that offends someone else becomes *their* problem, not ours.

Bias Does Not Equal Discrimination

One of the primary reasons it is uncomfortable to admit we have biases is because we think it means we hurt or exclude others intentionally. But bias is not a synonym for discrimination.

- A bias is a feeling, a preference or a perception that one thing or one group is better or worse than another. It is something that happens in your thinking or in your emotions. It influences your actions, but the bias is not actually what you do or say.

- Discrimination, on the other hand, is the behavior that results in a person or group being set apart in some way.

In the United States we typically equate discrimination with an individual or group being set apart in a negative way, i.e. being excluded, disrespected or harmed. But technically we are also practicing discrimination when we choose to set apart the talented and gifted students in a separate class or when we select the top 3 candidates for a "high potential" management program.

One is discrimination "against" a group or person. The other is discrimination "for" a group or person. Either way our biases (for or against) specific characteristics resulted in a discriminatory action.

Uncovering Your Biases

Since most people think discrimination against another group of people is morally or ethically wrong, most of us would prefer to believe we have no biases.

But in order to be an effective role-model for inclusion it is critical for every diversity champion to be acutely aware of ways his or her biases show up in daily behavior.

Only when you are aware of your biases are you then able to be alert and manage your unconscious responses to certain types of people.

The Implicit Bias Tests

Researchers and professors from several prestigious universities collaborated and created Project Implicit more than 10 years ago. Project Implicit includes a collection

72

of web-based tests that allow you to "experience the manner in which human minds display the effects of stereotypic and prejudicial associations acquired from their socio-cultural environment."

In other words, you can go to the website and participate in tests that show you what biases you have related to a number of different factors. There are tests related to a variety of diversity-related factors, including age, gender and ethnicity.

You Are Not Alone

All of us have biases. And our biases do affect the way we interact with others. Some of the findings observed after seven years of operating Project Implicit included:

- Implicit biases are pervasive. Over 80% of web respondents show implicit negativity toward the elderly compared to the young; 75-80% of self-identified Whites and Asians show an implicit preference for Whites rather than Blacks.

- People are often unaware of their implicit biases. Ordinary people, including the researchers who direct this project, are found to harbor negative associations to various social groups (i.e., implicit biases) even while honestly reporting that they regard themselves as lacking these biases.

- Implicit biases predict behavior. From simple acts of friendliness and inclusion to more consequential acts such as the evaluation of work quality, those

73

who are higher in implicit bias have been shown to display greater discrimination.

Champions for diversity and inclusion know they, like everyone else, have biases. Instead of deluding ourselves that biases don't exist, diversity champions focus on developing the ability to manage biases so they don't control our actions.

Get to know your biases so you can manage them. If you know what biases you have you can monitor your behavior and ensure you don't unintentionally disrespect others.

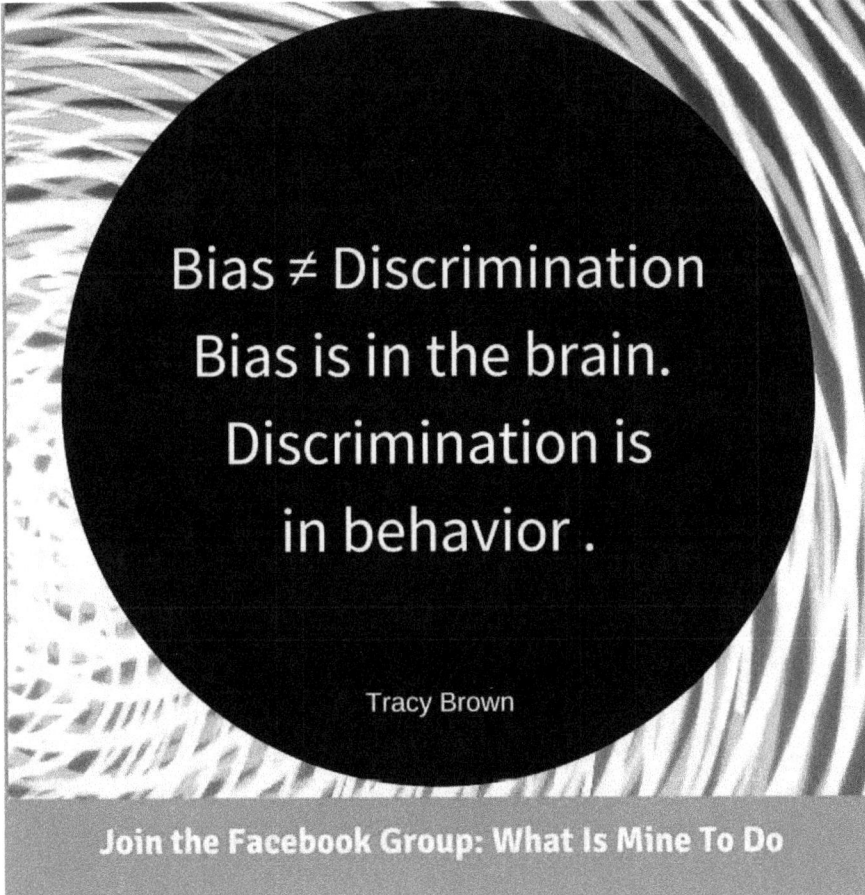

Bias ≠ Discrimination
Bias is in the brain.
Discrimination is
in behavior .

Tracy Brown

Join the Facebook Group: What Is Mine To Do

"We are all unique, and if that is not fulfilled, then something wonderful has been lost."

Martha Graham

Join the Facebook Group: What Is Mine To Do

The Melting Pot

the melting pot
never worked for me.
and so i made my own –
pot, that is.
and instead of melting,
it's cast in bronze …
that glows!

View differences as educational instead of frightening.

Tracy Brown

Join the Facebook Group: What Is Mine To Do

Intercultural Competence is a Learnable Skill

Most white people I know who are over the age of 45 and grew up in the United States were taught intercultural denial. As a black girl growing up during the civil rights movement I was taught intercultural survival. Younger adults in the U.S. have been taught intercultural awareness.

But denial, survival and awareness do not create workplaces or communities where rapidly increasing diversity can be easily transformed into respectful experiences and inclusive environments.

Intercultural competence is a learned skill.

One of my favorite models that helps diagnose intercultural activity is the *Developmental Model of Intercultural Sensitivity* (DMIS) by Dr. Milton Bennett.

The six stages of DMIS represent a set of perspectives with successively greater ability to understand and have a more positive experience of cultural difference.

Briefly, some characteristics of each stage are:

- **Denial**. Being comfortable with the familiar. Not anxious to complicate life with "cultural differences". Not noticing much cultural difference around you. Maintaining separation from others who are different.

- **Defense**. A strong commitment to one's own thoughts and feelings about culture and cultural

79

difference. Some distrust of cultural behavior or ideas that differ from one's own. Aware of other cultures around you, but with a relatively incomplete understanding of them and probably fairly strong negative feelings or stereotypes about some of them.

- **Minimization**. People from other cultures are pretty much like you, under the surface. Awareness that other cultures exist all around you, with some knowledge about differences in customs and celebrations. Not putting down other cultures. Treating other people as you would like to be treated.

- **Acceptance**. Aware of your own culture(s). See your own culture as just one of many ways of experiencing the world. Understanding that people from other cultures are as complex as yourself. Their ideas, feelings, and behavior may seem unusual, but you realize that their experience is just as rich as your own. Being curious about other cultures. Seeking opportunities to learn more about them.

- **Adaptation**. Recognizing the value of having more than one cultural perspective available to you. Able to "take the perspective" of another culture to understand or evaluate situations in either your own or another culture. Able to intentionally change your culturally based behavior to act in culturally appropriate ways outside your own culture.

- **Integration**. To varying extents, have integrated more than one cultural perspective, mindset, and behavior into one's identity and worldview. Able to move easily among cultures.

The first three stages are considered "ethnocentric" in that one's own culture is seen as the only culture or to varying extents the "better" culture.

The last three stages are considered "ethnorelative" in that one's own culture is seen as equal among many other cultures.

Using a model such as this simply encourages self-assessment that helps me set a clear intention for how I want to behave and helps me understand the feedback I might receive about something I did or said.

How might this model help you develop a higher level of intercultural competence?

"Many people think they are living by principles when they are just living by prejudices."

H B Jeffery

Join the Facebook Group: What Is Mine To Do

Fighting or Forwarding?

I was facilitating a 2-day retreat with a diversity council. There was one person in the group who I will refer to as "One Issue Wanda." We had been meeting for a day and a half and every comment "Wanda" made, every question she asked and every idea she offered was directly related to one specific identity group.

Finally, one of her colleagues raised his hand. When it was his turn to speak he got her attention and asked,

> *"Do you care about any employees in our organization who are from other ethnic groups?"*

Of course her answer was,

> *"Yes, I care about all employees."*

He then followed up with,

> *"So why do you only speak about what needs to be done for employees in your own ethnic group?"*

She paused and said,

> *"Well the only group I know anything about is my own. And somebody has to speak up for us."*

There was complete silence in the room. Then the person sitting next to her said,

> *"I am a white woman. If every comment I made and every question I asked was about white people you would say I was being racist. That's not fair."*

Another employee at the next table quickly chimed in,

> *"You expect me to learn about your ethnic group and I'm happy to do so. But aren't you also supposed to*

83

learn about all of ours? We are all learning together aren't we?"

This exchange led into a really deep and meaningful conversation about what it takes to be inclusive. The conversation quickly went beyond ethnicity and included the group's desire to ensure inclusion of employees based on sexual orientation, physical (dis)ability, age and other distinctions. Frustrations were shared and courageous statements about going beyond individual experience were made.

One of the most powerful comments came from "Wanda" a little later in the dialogue when she said,

> *"I guess I've just always believed you all didn't really care about me and I needed to fight tooth and nail to get anything done. But as I listen to you now, and when I think about our meetings over the past year, I know that's not true."*

What about you? Do you think the only way to be a champion for diversity is to put on your battle gear for every conversation? Or do you realize that being inclusive is a learning opportunity where everyone becomes an ally for everyone else?

For a day and a half this group had some very important conversations and a lot of valuable information was shared. But it was during the final 3 hours of their retreat that new bridges were built, new expectations were agreed to and they became a team more fully able to model equity and inclusion for all.

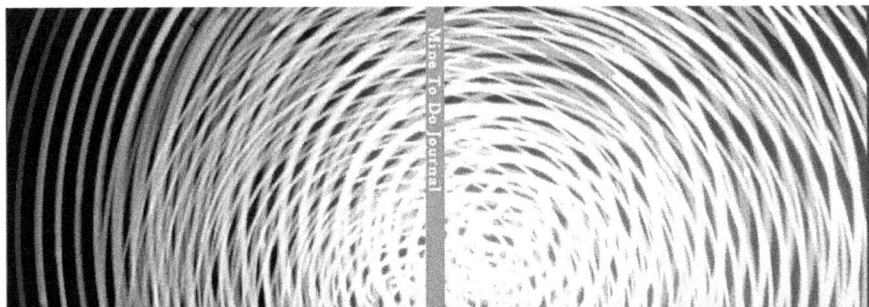

Tips for Allies

Mine To Do Journal

inspire clarity.
encourage acceptance.
create partnerships.
work with intention.

Tracy Brown

Join the Facebook Group: What Is Mine To Do

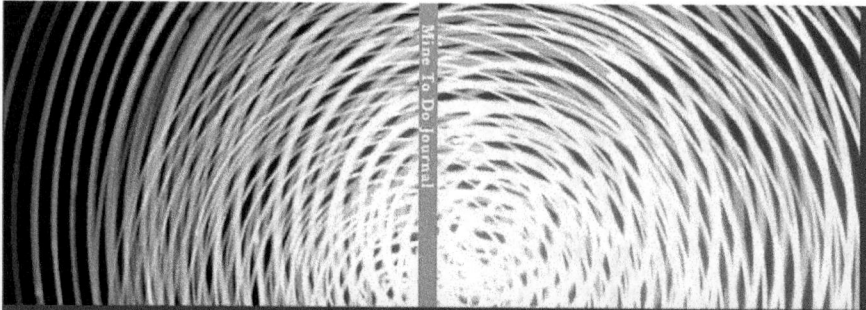

Tips for Allies

inspire change.
encourage respect.
create opportunity.
work selflessly.

Tracy Brown

Join the Facebook Group: What Is Mine To Do

Do You Like Me?

A few weeks ago a woman, let's call her Sally, looked at me and asked, "You don't like me very much do you? Is there anything I've done or said that offended you?"

Now, from a diversity and inclusion perspective, the second sentence is actually a really good one. However, in this case, the assumption that I didn't like Sally was way off base.

I neither like nor dislike Sally. I know her. I've been in a few meetings with her. We've been in some small group discussions and got along just fine. When we pass in the hallways we stop and greet each other. I think she's cool enough and her perspective is interesting to me. But there has never been any social interaction, i.e. getting to know each other over meals or going to events together, etc. And until the moment she asked me that question I had not spent even 5 seconds wondering whether I liked her or not.

I am ALWAYS shocked when someone I have a business relationship with asks me if I like them. For me, liking people I work with (or having people I work with like me) is not a primary requirement. Qualifications and skills are my #1 consideration. Respect is a very close #2. Having the resources required to get the job done is #3.
And *maybe* liking each other comes in at #4. (But if I were to sit here and think a minute there might be other items that would move into the #4 spot.)

When I was the chief HR officer for an organization that was filling lots of positions because of rapid growth I would often talk with managers and supervisors whose primary reason to hire - or fire - an employee was based on how much liked (or disliked) the person. Of course they would never say that. Instead they would use code language like:

1. Of the three finalists, Mary will just fit in better.

2. Well, yes, there are other employees who have been late the same number of times but Dave is just so difficult to work with. We can replace him with someone who fits in better with the team.

3. I'm not sure Laura is the right candidate; she has young children so she probably won't be able to join us after work for happy hour very often and that's a part of why we get along so well.

4. I've never really felt comfortable with Greg from the beginning. So let's cut our losses and start over with someone new.

Of course I know every supervisor or manager isn't going to like every person they work with. But managers are hired to lead - not like - the entire team. This means:

- You hire for skills, talents, experiences and perspectives that enhance the team's ability to not just achieve goals but to exceed expectations

- You provide personal and professional development opportunities to every member of your team.

- You recruit and promote based on performance, not personality.

- You manage your own biases, hold yourself to a higher standard of respect and model inclusive behaviors.

I had a great conversation with Sally. I asked her what made her think I didn't like her. I asked her why it felt important for her that I like her. I sincerely wanted to understand what was missing in our interaction that would make her feel more comfortable in our ongoing relationship. I answered questions she had and also shared more about my needs and expectations.

In a conversation that lasted less than 15 minutes we both walked away with mutual respect and understanding. It's not likely we'll ever be friends socially but I have no doubt we can work together on project teams and other activities with ease and grace.

I am grateful she was able to express her fear or concern that I didn't like her. She actually thought because I didn't like her I might not support her growth or recommend her for other opportunities. She thought that not because of anything I had done, but because other people she had worked with in the past used the phrase, "Well I just think someone else would be a better fit." And the person they selected or promoted was someone who was perceived to be their "buddy" or their "best friend" on the team.

Let's all hold ourselves to a higher standard than that. Let's all redefine "fit" in a multidimensional way that is led by skills and talents. Let's all be willing to be a little more uncomfortable in order to create a comfortable environment for others around us.

Tips for Allies

inspire curiosity.
encourage collaboration.
create something new.
work on it everyday.

Tracy Brown

Join the Facebook Group: What Is Mine To Do

White Guys Are Not the Enemy

In many diversity initiatives it seems as if white men are the bad guys, responsible for all the bad things that have ever happened to white women and people of color.

But in order to have a successful diversity initiative your organization must engage white men and include their perspectives.

All white men do not have the same experiences, perspectives, priorities, needs, values or beliefs. So why do so many inclusion initiatives treat white men, as a group, as if they are all the same and are all the enemy?

Most organizations that have received recognition for their commitment to diversity and inclusion have been led by white men. Clearly these men were motivated and willing to commit resources to diversity and inclusion. What made them different?

In every civil rights effort there have been white men who stood up to express the importance of fair treatment for people who didn't look like them, or practice the same religion, or share the same ethnicity.

So white men, as a whole, are not the problem.

In the United States many cultural norms (in life and in business) have historically been based on the perceived needs and preferences of white, Christian, heterosexual, physically-able men. But that should be no surprise since historically people with these five characteristics comprised the majority of people in leadership and decision-making positions.

91

It is important to understand the traditional or historical culture, even as we recognize the culture in the U.S. has been changing more rapidly than ever before. Diversity initiatives in corporations and associations should recognize the cultural norms of the past, have a clear vision for the desired cultural norms of the future, and be focused on building the bridge between those two.

One of the historical dominant culture values is individualism. So, in general, white men are more likely to value being seen as an individual and are more likely to step up to a leadership role on diversity issues if they see an opportunity to be recognized as an individual who sets a new standard or who will be recognized as a role-model.

Also remember that not all white men operate from the dominant culture. For example, we frequently hear from white men who are gay that even though they have been exposed to the norms of the dominant culture they often don't operate totally within those guidelines. They often report more affinity with people of color because they have also experienced prejudice, discomfort and exclusion.

Finally, encourage the white men in your organization to become allies to white women and people of color.

Give white men the same respect, and the same benefit of the doubt, and the same opportunities to contribute to your diversity initiative, as everyone else.

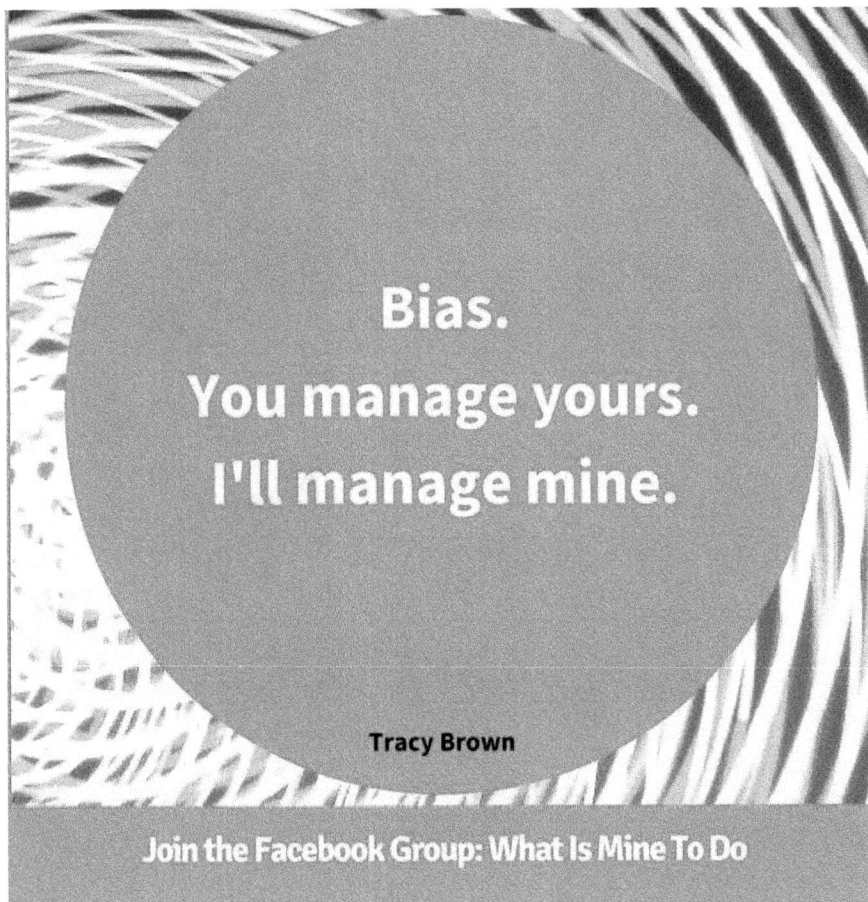

Bias.
You manage yours.
I'll manage mine.

Tracy Brown

Join the Facebook Group: What Is Mine To Do

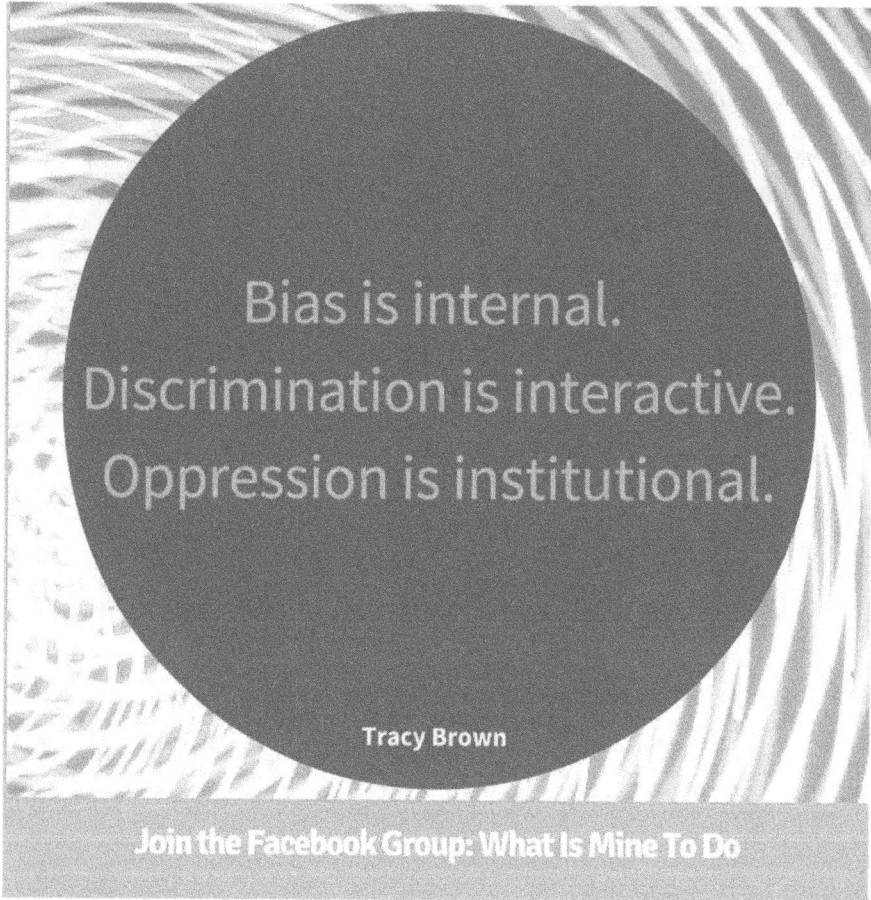

Bias is internal.
Discrimination is interactive.
Oppression is institutional.

Tracy Brown

Join the Facebook Group: What Is Mine To Do

Discomfort is No Excuse for Disrespect

When we are uncomfortable with others it often shows up in what we way about them in our conversations with others. Without thinking we say inappropriate comments like:

- "I've never been around people from that background so I just avoid her."

- "They shouldn't be allowed to speak Spanish at work. I don't know what they are saying. They could be talking about me."

- "You'd better take your lunch early; the [fill in the blank] employees generally take over the break room about 12:15p and you don't want to be in there with them."

- "I heard the new sales supervisor they hired is gay. You can bet I won't be going to any closed door meetings in his office or riding with him on sales calls.

There are four things that are especially troubling about these kinds of statements.

1. None of them are based on our individual interaction with the people we are passing judgment on.

2. None of them take into account the skills, talents or work-related contributions of the individual(s) we are referring to.

95

3. None of them would likely be said directly to the person or group being referred to.

4. None of them are meant to be offensive; the person is simply expressing his or her opinion or assumption as if it is fact.

I often say to people in my workshops that at least 85% of the time when offensive or inappropriate comments are made it is unintentional. This is a made up statistic -- but it is accurate based on my actual experience working in, and working with, organizations my entire adult life.

My Comments About You Are Really About Me

Often people make comments based on their desire to feel comfortable and the fact that most of the time they find themselves interacting with people they are similar to or comfortable with.

In the workplace, however, most of us don't get to personally choose everyone we work with. Most of us encounter people from different backgrounds, different age groups, different ethnic groups and different communication styles at work more than in any other part of our lives.

So when we make comments that judge, criticize or condemn others (based on characteristics related to their group identity) it usually isn't about them. It is usually about our own lack of information, limited exposure or hidden fears.

I personally view all this diversity as an opportunity to explore more ways of life than my own and I find it pretty interesting. (So it's no wonder I live and breathe diversity

96

and inclusion, right?) But for many people diversity can be a source of irritation, a source of confusion, and yes ... a source of discomfort.

What to Do?

So the first thing to do is to realize that it is natural to feel discomfort when you encounter people who are different from you in some significant way. You can't predict what they will do or how they will do it. You may not know their needs or expectations. And in the workplace, where you are focused on getting results, this can be unsettling.

The next thing to do is to accept that everyone is not like you and that is a good thing. One of the big advantage of being a part of a workforce where there is lots of diversity is the opportunity to view problems from different angles and generate a broader list of possible solutions.

Another advantage diversity offers in the workplace is the ability it provides for you and your team to anticipate and respond to a wider variety of customers who represent groups and perspectives you, as an individual, may not be exposed to. Look for the ways that diversity can serve as a resource to make your job and your experience at work more successful.

And, if you are willing to change your assumptions, reach out and develop a relationship with someone from the group you previously judged or criticized. The biggest antidote to generalizing an entire group is to have personal relationships with someone who is a member of that group. It's the best reminder that everyone is an individual, sometimes sharing the characteristics of the group and sometimes not.

Monitor Your Behavior and the Comments You Make

When you realize you are criticizing a person (or group of people) because of something they do that you aren't comfortable with, stop.

- Remind yourself that you weren't hired to judge them; you were hired to work with them to accomplish a goal.

- Remind yourself that to them, you might be the one who is "different" in a way they are unfamiliar with.

- Remind yourself that your view of the world isn't the only (or best) view of the world.

- Remind yourself that your discomfort with them is not an acceptable excuse for behaving or speaking in disrespectful ways.

When I am designing a seminar, workshop or teleseminar for clients and ask them what three things they want our training to include, the list almost always includes something related to reducing inappropriate comments made by employees. Do your part to stop this trend in your organization.

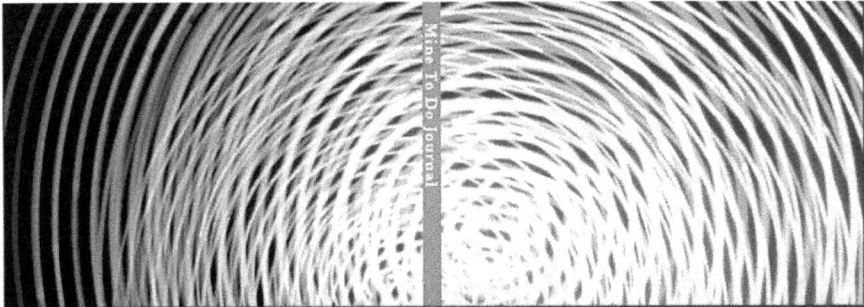

Tips for Allies

indict or inspire?

enforce or encourage?

complain or create?

whine or work?

(your choice)

Tracy Brown

Join the Facebook Group: What Is Mine To Do

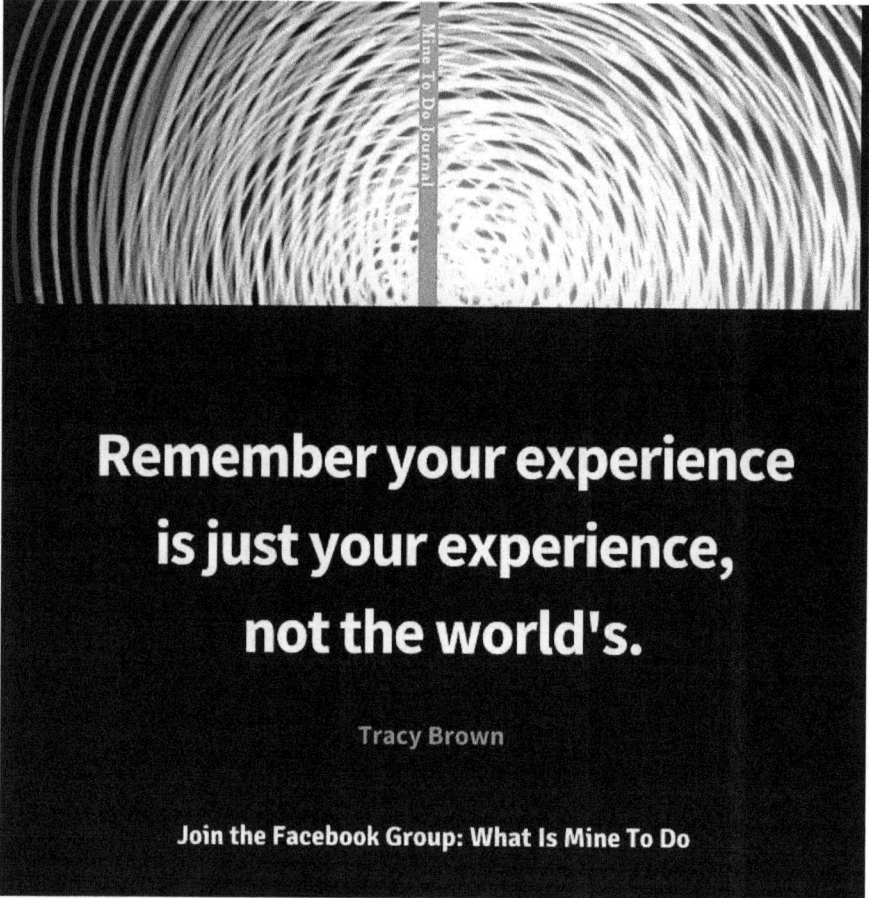

Mine To Do Journal

Remember your experience is just your experience, not the world's.

Tracy Brown

Join the Facebook Group: What Is Mine To Do

Essential Tools

[excerpts from the book, Breaking the Barrier of Bias: The Subtle Influence of Bias and What You Can Do about It" by Tracy Brown]

Here are eight must-have tools in your Breaking the Barrier of Bias Tool Kit.

1. One of the first skill building tools you should seek out in your quest to beak the barrier of bias is to *learn to confront others in a positive way.*

2. Another tool you should carry in your tool it is the skill of *active listening*. Learn to paraphrase. Learn to restate the point the other person is making until you can get them to acknowledge you have really heard their point.

3. *Never argue with someone about right and wrong* when you're talking about bias and differences. Focus instead on possibility and personal meaning.

4. Don't strive for agreement. *Work hard for understanding.*

5. *Be willing to share your own assumptions* as much as you solicit the assumptions of others. When you begin to share what you thought a specific situation or word, or action, meant, the other person will be encouraged to share on the same level. You then become peers in the interaction. You can become allies, working together to find a solution (instead of enemies fighting to be right, or to prove the other person wrong).

6. Make a commitment to *speak up* or don't complain later. Silence usually is interpreted as acceptance or agreement.

101

7. Learn to *let someone know they have offended you without labeling them,* and without calling hem negative names. Describe the behavior, or the specific content of what they said which was offensive and explain why. Criticizing them without explaining what was offensive does not help them change.

8. *Practice asking questions,* rather than making statements. Asking someone, "Do you realize that could be considered an offensive statement?" is much more effective than saying, "There you go again, making those offensive statements. You always do that!"

These are just a few of the most important tools you should carry in your Breaking the Barrier of Bias tool kit!

Everyone is kneaded out of the same dough, but not baked in the same oven

Yiddish Proverb

Join the Facebook Group: What Is Mine To Do

"Your daily behavior reveals your deepest beliefs."

Tracy Brown

Join the Facebook Group: What Is Mine To Do

Diversity Cop or Diversity Coach?

Do people think of you as a "Diversity Cop" who is focused on enforcing the law, finding their mistakes, or changing their values?

Would you prefer people to think of you as a "Diversity Coach" who is focused on encouraging effective behavior, finding solutions to common challenges, and growing an inclusive culture?

Of course there are times when it is necessary to be a "diversity cop". If rules or policies are intentionally ignored or when discrimination is evident, being a diversity cop is appropriate.

But for all the times when it is more helpful to be a diversity coach, here are six things you must do to develop your ability to be a great coach for diversity and inclusion.

1. REGULAR SELF ASSESSMENT. Are you modeling inclusive behavior? What have you changed in the past year? Who are your allies? Regularly look in the mirror and identify what is working and what needs to change in order for you to be effective as a diversity champion.

2. PRACTICE THE SKILLS AND BEHAVIORS. It is difficult to coach others to handle situations you don't have the ability to handle yourself. A football coach doesn't have to have personal experience in every position on the team to be a great coach. But a part of his ability to be successful comes from his experience playing the game or being on the field

105

thousands of times. As a diversity coach you too must have skills you can teach and transfer to others.

3. STUDY THE TOPIC. What have you read or done lately that taught you something new about diversity or inclusion? Develop the discipline to read, listen to audio programs, or take a class on a regular basis. Scan the newspaper or the internet at least weekly for related stories.

4. BE AN ALLY TO OTHERS. Let people from different identity groups know you are an ally to them. Attend events. Initiate one-on-one conversations. Volunteer.

5. PRACTICE NONDEFENSIVE RESPONSES. Take in what people are saying without reacting emotionally. Even when someone is giving you personal feedback, focus on understanding their comments from their perspective. And always express appreciation for feedback that is difficult to take in. (If it's hard for you to hear it, it's probably equally hard for the person to give it.)

6. APPLY EXTRAORDINARY LISTENING SKILLS. Ask good questions but listen more than you speak. Listen not only for meaning but also for mood. Listen for feelings as well as facts.

These six tasks, applied on a consistent basis, will set you up to be an effective and sought after coach for diversity and inclusion. And, as Gandhi said, "Be the change you wish to see in the world."

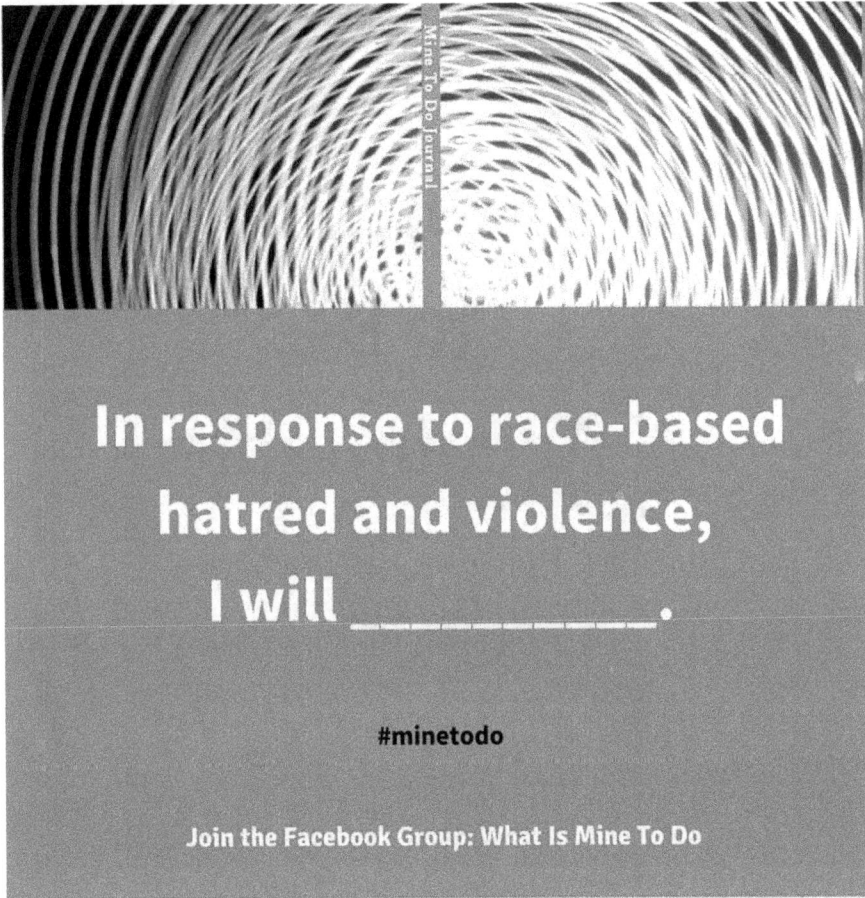

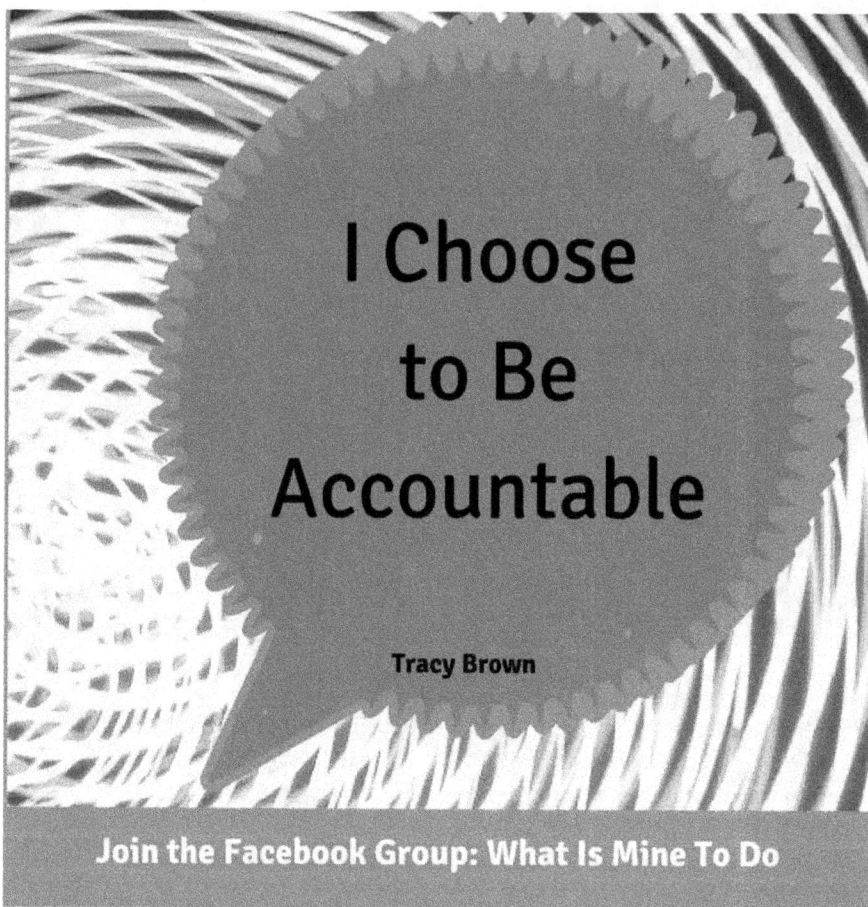

I Choose

My belief in the power of mutual respect inspires certain behaviors.
My commitment to respect and equity requires consistent action.
And so, I choose my path and hold myself to a higher standard.

I choose to be respectful.

I choose to be fair.

I choose to remember everyone has a story I may never know.

I choose to believe that harmony is possible.

I choose to listen for understanding not agreement.

I choose to quietly do the right thing.

I choose to be relentless in my expectation for equity.

I choose to believe it is my responsibility to be an example of love in the world.

I choose to accept that I will make mistakes.

I choose to remember that I can recover from any mistakes I make.

I choose to be grateful for having a voice and a vision.

I choose to welcome people who are not like me into my world, my church, my school, my workplace and my home.

I choose to challenge the status quo.

I choose to believe there is a better way to live together in harmony.

I choose to question assumptions and deny stereotypes.

I choose to recognize my own biases and manage them.

I choose to partner with others who want to make a positive difference.

I choose to accept that whether or not others agree with me is not my business.

I choose to study and learn.

I choose to be in service to a higher vision.

I choose to be an encourager.

I choose to stand firmly committed to mutual respect.

I choose to fight for a world that is loving instead of fighting against those who hate and harm.

I choose to use spiritual practice to ground me.

I choose to draw attention to unfair practices and behaviors.

I choose to be grateful for all I have experienced.

I choose to be grateful for all I have learned.

I choose to give myself a "learners' permit" and remember I will never know all there is to know.

I choose to accept that everyone has a unique personality and an individually perfect path.

I choose to remember that my way is not the only way.

I choose to give attention to the good I want to see more of in the world.

I choose to release all fear of people who seem to be strong because of power or politics.

I choose to believe turning the other cheek means showing a different way of responding.

I choose to do what I can do wherever I am with the people I come into contact with.

I choose to be grateful for every opportunity to confront bias and discrimination.

I choose to set a higher standard for myself and for society.

I choose to know that there is a power for good and that power needs me to demonstrate its value.

I choose to be grateful for the inner peace that allows me to accept others.

I choose to talk to people who are not like me.

I choose to speak constantly about the potential for love and respect to become the norm.

I choose to assume positive intent.

I choose to view others as my equal.

I choose to check my ego at the door and remember it's not all about me.

I choose to stand side-by-side with anyone who is oppressed or persecuted or excluded because of the color of their skin.

I choose to hang out with winners instead of whiners.

I choose to remember that people who are hurting are most likely to hurt others.

I choose to develop and share simple and practical solutions to common misunderstandings.

I choose to offer hope to the hopeless.

I choose to inspire myself and others to believe in a higher standard for our treatment of people.

I choose to speak the names of heroes and sheroes instead of focusing on those who hurt and harm.

I choose to focus on change in my sphere of control.

I choose to believe if everyone focused on change in their individual sphere of control the entire world would change rapidly.

I choose to believe that politicians and policy are impotent in the face of a population that demands peace and respect.

I choose to believe that life is meant to be a peaceful, joyful journey.

I choose to release my need for approval and simply do what I know to be right and fair.

I choose to be grateful for the wisdom to understand there is a better way to live.

I choose to accept others where they are.

I choose to believe that everyone, including me, is always growing and expanding.

I choose to know that "the right thing" is always the right thing. It is not circumstantial.

I choose to remember that forgiveness is a gift I give myself and in no way condones the behavior of others.

I choose to hold myself accountable.

I choose to help others on this journey toward mutual respect.

I choose to teach what I know to those who can benefit.

I choose to focus on what I want instead of what I don't want.

I choose to grow.

I choose to be grateful for the courage to speak up.

I choose to be an example of someone who isn't perfect but keeps moving forward anyway.

I choose to remember I am not doing this alone.

I choose to point out progress more than I highlight pain.

I choose to expect excellence from everyone regardless of the color of their skin.

I choose to believe that diversity is God's design and not an accident or mistake.

I choose to remember I am not fighting against anything; I am fighting FOR something important.

I choose to remember that no one else can do what is mine to do. I must do my part for the world to change.

About the Author

TRACY BROWN

Tracy@TracyBrown.com

Tracy Brown is shifting the conversation about diversity and inclusion from politics and personality to relationships and productivity.

Let her help you discover – and then implement – whatever is yours to do to transform your life or your workplace.

- Corporations and Associations: Diversity and Inclusion Strategy and Skill Building: www.Diversity-Strategy.com

- Diversity/Inclusion for Spiritual Communities: www.StainedGlassSpirit.net

115

Diversity Champions™

Diversity Champions Unleashed
27 Lessons to Help You Be a Better Champion for Diversity and Inclusion

This web-based course is designed to:
- equip you with knowledge about specific behaviors, resources and tactics you can use to be a champion for diversity and inclusion
- encourage you to take appropriate risks and set higher standards for your behavior as a champion for diversity and inclusion
- empower you to take personal responsibility for being a champion for diversity and inclusion in your workplace or community

There are 27 modules / lessons. Each one includes either educational models and facts or a self-directed activity designed to help you strengthen your skills. The content has recently been updated so you'll find links to resources you can use to expand your knowledge and update your tool kit!

You can add a new lesson each day for 27 days ... or you can set your own pace. But no matter what schedule you choose, you are not going through the course alone. Anytime you have questions or comments you can post them to the discussion board for response or contact me directly.

If you are ready to be a more effect champion for diversity and inclusion in the workplace and beyond, this course will help you achieve your goal!

STAINED GLASS SPIRIT
Where Many Are One

Oneness not Sameness

Can We Have Oneness in a World Where There's So Much Diversity?

No two of us are the same. Ernest Holmes tells us, "The Universal is Infinite: the possibility of differentiating is limitless." The Unity Principles remind us "each person is a unique expression of God created with sacred worth."

So the vast diversity in humanity is not an accident. Our differences actually represent the unlimited expression of Life.

If you are ready to move beyond political barriers and societal norms to create a world that works for everyone what's your next step? How do spiritual principles inspire you? How might spiritual practices sustain you?

Come explore how we can live the spiritual principle of Oneness and still honor the diversity of the people we live, work and worship with.

This class can be offered online or in person.

DIVERSITY TRENDS
FROM BIAS TO BRIDGES

STAINED GLASS SPIRIT
Where Many Are One

DISCUSSING™
DIVERSITY

DIVERSITY
TOOLKIT
TUNE + UP
™

strategy
assume positive intent
respect
reconciliation
listening
communication reinvention
dialogue
future focused
love
intentionally inclusive
forgiveness
retain
action
diversity inquiry
relationships
inclusion

Inspiring Quotations

Allow these additional quotations to inspire you or to share them with others. You can also use them as discussion starters when you want to have a dialogue about your commitment to building a community based on respect and fairness.

And, if you really love quotations, purchase the *Mine to Do Journal*. It includes more than 125 quotes with plenty of room to write or draw as you reflect on how the quotations inspire or inform you.

The danger is that people may mistake what is basically a change of vocabulary for a change in behavior, practices and attitudes.
While practically all Americans have learned to talk inoffensively, not enough have learned to think differently or to act positively.
Whitney Young

Don't tolerate me as different. Accept me as part of the spectrum of normalcy.
Ann Northrop

The price of hating other human beings is loving oneself less.
Eldridge Cleaver

There is a difference between conversations about what's politically correct and conversations about issues of human respect and dignity.
Chris Terry

Mine to Do: Responding to Race-Based Hatred and Violence

*Developing acceptance requires you to
get out of your comfort zone.*
Lenora Billings-Harris

*The world in which you were born is just one
model of reality. Other cultures are not failed
attempts at being you; they are unique
manifestations of the human spirit.*
Wade Davis

*Begin challenging your own assumptions. Your
assumptions are your windows on the world. Scrub
them off every once in a while, or the light
won't come in.*
Alan Alda

*I don't accept the world the way it works. I take on
the world. I want to make the world the
way it should be.*
Bernice Johnson Reagon

*While I know myself as a creation of God, I am also
obligated to realize and remember that everyone
else and everything else are also God's creation.*
Maya Angelou

In true dialogue, both sides are willing to change.
Thich Nhat Hanh

*Our unconscious biases build barriers between us
and the people we meet every day. When we
are unaware of the ways we demonstrate our
biases, we miss opportunities to build
bridges with people.*
Tracy Brown

Mine to Do: Responding to Race-Based Hatred and Violence

*We awaken in others the same attitude of mind
we hold toward them.*
Elbert Hubbard

*There are no degrees of human freedom or human
dignity. Either a man respects another as a person
or he does not.*
James Cone

*Progress lies not in enhancing what is, but in
advancing toward what will be.*
Kahlil Gibran

*We all do 'do, re, mi,' but you have got to find the
other notes yourself.*
Louis Armstrong

*The world as we see it is only the world as we see
it. Others may see it differently.*
Albert Einstein

People only see what they are prepared to see.
Ralph Waldo Emerson

*In Germany they first came for the communists and
I didn't speak up because I wasn't a communist.
Then they came for the Jews and I didn't speak up
because I wasn't a Jew. Then they came for the
trade unionists and I didn't speak up because I
wasn't a trade unionist. Then they came for the
Catholics and I didn't speak up because I wasn't a
Catholic. Then they came for me – and by that time
there was nobody left to speak up.*
Martin Niemöller

Mine to Do: Responding to Race-Based Hatred and Violence

Instead of changing addresses, address the issue.
Eric Allenbough

We are, of course, a nation of differences. Those differences are the source of our strength.
Jimmy Carter

To live anywhere in the world today and be against equality because of race or color is like living in Alaska and being against snow.
William Faulkner

Prejudice is like a hair across your cheek. You can't see it, you can't find it with your fingers, but you keep brushing at it because the feel of it is irritating.
Marian Anderson

We all should know that diversity makes for a rich tapestry. And we must understand that all the threads of the tapestry are equal in value no matter what their color.
Maya Angelou

If you judge people, you do not have time to love them.
Mother Teresa

Creating an environment where diversity is valued does NOT mean making different rules for each person or group. The challenge is making everyone feel valued while encouraging unique approaches and skills
Tracy Brown

Mine to Do: Responding to Race-Based Hatred and Violence

*I am not a slave of the slavery that dehumanized
my ancestors.*
Frantz Fanon

*Choose your friends by their character and your
socks by their color. Choosing your socks by their
character makes no sense, and choosing your
friends by their color is unthinkable.*
Anonymous

*Unity and diversity are not adversarial but, rather,
complementary parts of a unified whole.*
Marianne Williamson

*This (diversity work) is a fight for the
soul of our country.*
Maria Hinojosa

*Ideologies separate us.
Dreams and anguish bring us together.*
Eugene Ionesco

*If civilization is to survive, we must cultivate the
science of human relationships: the ability of all
peoples, of all kinds, to live together, in the same
world, at peace.*
Franklin D. Roosevelt

*We have flown the air like birds and swum the sea
like fishes, but have yet to learn the simple act of
walking the earth like brothers.*
Martin Luther King, Jr.

Mine to Do: Responding to Race-Based Hatred and Violence

None of us is responsible for the complexion of his skin. This fact of nature offers no clue to the character or quality of the person underneath.
Marian Anderson

Sustained engagement around race is also threatened by the profoundly American impulse to treat one another as if we were individuals first, last and only.
Harlon Dalton

An inch of progress is worth more than a yard of complaint.
Booker T Washington

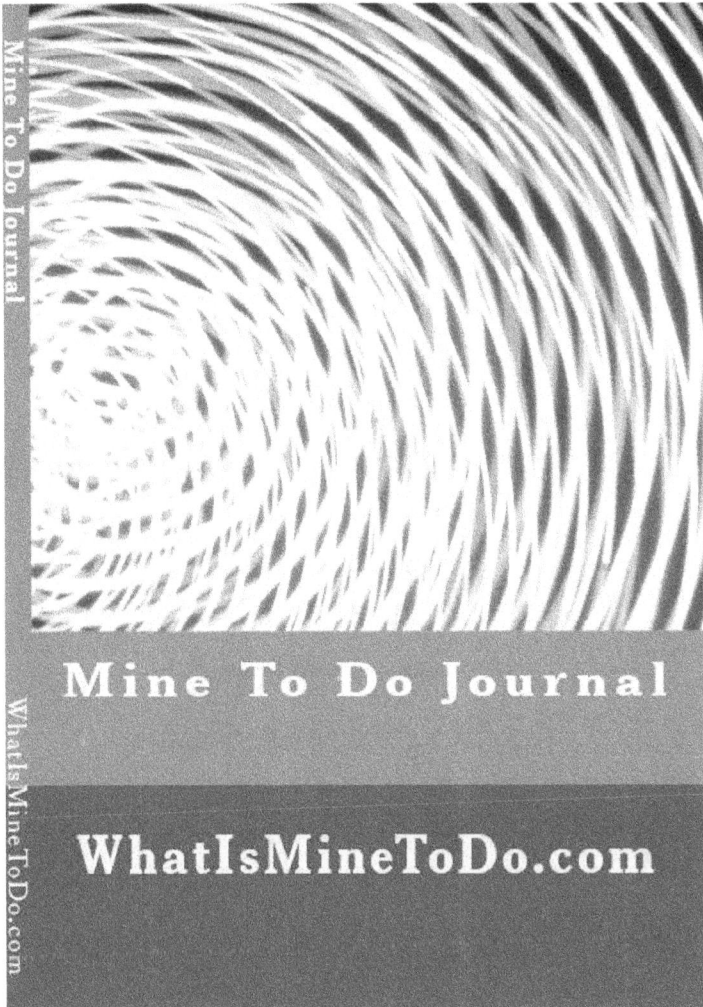

Purchase the "Mine to Do" Journal on Amazon.com

What will YOU do to stop
race-based hatred and violence?

#minetodo

join the facebook group:
"what is mine to do"

Facebook.com/groups/minetodo/

www.WhatIsMineToDo.com

www.ingramcontent.com/pod-product-compliance
Lightning Source LLC
Chambersburg PA
CBHW081417270326
41931CB00015B/3309